End-of-Term Projects

Projects

A package of stories and
curriculum-related activities

Helen Sonnet

End-of-Term Projects

ISBN 13: 978 1 85503 492 1

MT 11815

© Helen Sonnet

All illustrations by Clare Jarvis

All rights reserved

First published 2011

Printed in the UK for LDA by Page Bros, Norwich

LDA, Findel Education, Hyde Buildings, Ashton Road, Hyde, Cheshire, SK14 4SH

Contents

Introduction

The last week of term can be a stressful time for teachers. There are often myriad jobs to finish as well as preparations for the new term ahead to make. The curriculum work has perhaps been completed and it may seem an onerous task to plan meaningful lessons for the final week.

I have seen many colleagues struggle to find their classes appropriate work for this time. They often end up producing tasks that are unrelated and little better than time fillers. I decided that a resource was needed to fill the gap and provide teachers with a week of related, appropriate tasks that were also fun and engaging. Hence this book!

It provides six different themes of work, each designed to last for one week and to provide interest, enjoyment and meaningful, related tasks for the children. Photocopiable pages are included so that very little preparatory work is involved, thus freeing up the teacher for the pressing duties to be completed.

Each theme includes a story in five chapters, one for each day of the week, with a follow-up activity for each chapter. The story chapters are at the front of each section, followed by related tasks under these headings: Follow-up work for each chapter, Ideas for maths work, Science activities, Other activities (puzzles, board games etc.), Active games and Art. While the themes and activities have been selected for enjoyment, there is a wealth of knowledge supplied – provided in, for example, historical and geographical facts. These, together with opportunities to practise literacy and numeracy skills, ensure that the activities are worthwhile from an educational point of view.

Teachers may use the whole scheme of work for each theme, or dip into the section and choose the activities they prefer. Where necessary, the activities are graded for different levels of attainment or become progressively more difficult, allowing children of varying ages and capabilities to follow the same worksheet, and there are even opportunities for high attainers to devise their own content.

There are indications in the text of where it would be advisable to select mixed-ability pairs or groups, enabling children who are more able to help those on a lower level of attainment.

The engaging themes will stimulate the children's interest and imagination and prompt them to investigate the topics further, using other sources of information available to them.

I hope that this resource will enable both children and their teachers to find the last week of term enjoyable and rewarding.

The Mystery of Southfield House

A tale of mystery and intrigue
set in a Victorian villa

Chapter 1

As their car turned the corner of the gravel drive, Joe and Elena and even their dog Barney pressed their noses against the car window in eager anticipation of the first sighting of their holiday home.

This had been a last-minute booking of a property through a friend of their father's who had a holiday rental business. Southfield House had only just become available and there were no pictures printed yet, so the two children had discussed its possibilities on the long journey. Their hopes were now wavering between a kind of mini-castle and a charming thatched cottage. In fact, the house, when it came into view, was neither. It was a rather dull-looking grey stone Victorian villa and, quite frankly, a bit of a disappointment.

Once inside, the children bagged adjoining bedrooms at the back of the house. Elena unpacked her case, then joined Joe in the next room. He was looking out of the window and called her over to join him. "Look at this garden, Elena," he said. "It's huge."

"Oh, wow!" his sister breathed as she looked out. "C'mon, let's go and explore."

Stepping outside the French windows in the lounge, the children found themselves on a paved area, set with table and chairs, that stretched the entire width of the house. Beyond this, flower beds stocked with a variety of perennials displayed a riot of colours and bordered a neat lawn. Further away still were a selection of mature fruit trees in a small orchard. Here the children discovered a rope swing and a viewing platform attached to the sturdy branches of the biggest and oldest tree. In the corner of the orchard was a very dilapidated summer house that did not look in the least inviting.

They spent a happy couple of hours climbing the trees, playing hide-and-seek and then Pirates, while Barney snuffled round the garden savouring all the new and exciting scents. Eventually, feeling hungry and thirsty, they decided to return to the house for something to eat and drink. As they made their way back down the path, Elena noticed an archway in the hedge to her right. A climbing rose with deep red blooms trailed up and over the arch, and beyond this she caught a glimpse of further greenery.

"I wonder what's in there," she said to Joe.

"Oh, we can look later," he replied. "C'mon, I'm starving. I'll race you back to the house." With that he sprinted off. Elena was about to follow, but then her curiosity got the better of her and she slipped through the rose archway.

A small, well-tended garden met her eyes. In the centre stood a rather chipped stone statue. Radiating out from this were six areas filled with sweet-smelling lavender, creating a circular garden. A path bordered the circumference of this circle and beyond this ran a gravelled area. The gravelled area seemed to be divided into a number of plots, each of which was decorated in a different way. One had a design in smooth, round pebbles, another in lumps of quartz and a third in shells. Elena was drawn to the shell pattern. A large conch shell formed the centrepiece and was surrounded by a selection of smaller shells. It was so pretty that Elena decided to take some of the shells to show her mother, meaning to replace them afterwards.

Elena awoke from sleep that night to a bright light pouring into her window through a gap in the curtains. A large, silvery moon was shining directly into her eyes. She slipped out of bed and crossed the room, intending to close the curtains and, while doing so, glanced down into the garden. A sudden movement caught her attention. She saw the figure of a woman wearing a long, pale garment, who appeared to be searching the garden for something. Who on earth was she and what was she doing there in the middle of the night?

Elena ran into the next bedroom and shook Joe roughly awake. "Quick," she said, "Come and look, someone's in our garden."

Joe scrambled out of bed and pulled back one of his curtains. The movement caught the attention of the woman and she looked up at the window. The children noted a pale face with light-coloured hair drawn back into a bun at the nape of her neck. Seeing their faces peering down at her, the mysterious woman turned on her heel and began to walk swiftly down the garden towards the orchard.

"Come on," shouted Joe as he raced out of the bedroom and down the stairs. "Let's find out what she's doing."

Slipping on their shoes by the back door and calling Barney, the children ran out of the house and down the garden in the direction the woman had taken. The moonlight was so bright that it seemed almost like daylight, and the children could see the whole garden clearly.

When they reached the orchard, there was no sign of the intruder and no evidence of a route out of the garden.

"She's not here," whispered Joe. "She can't have doubled back as we'd have seen her and there's no way out of here, so where is she? She's just vanished."

Chapter 2

The two children stood in the orchard, mystified by the woman's disappearance. Elena was the first to break the silence. "Perhaps she was a ghost. I don't like this, Joe, it's spooky and I'm scared. Let's go back indoors."

Before Joe could protest, Elena set off at a fast walk towards the house. Once inside and feeling safe again, she relaxed a little. Turning to Joe, she said, "She has to be a ghost, don't you see? There's no other explanation. She just vanished into thin air."

"Well, I don't believe in ghosts," Joe told her. "We'll investigate again in the morning when it's light and we can see properly."

Although the two children went back to bed, neither of them slept very well. There were too many thoughts churning through their minds as they tried to think of an explanation for the night's mysterious events, each one seeming more improbable than the last.

They were both glad when morning arrived and they could meet up again and discuss their thoughts over breakfast.

"If she wasn't a ghost," said Elena, "then who could she be, and what was she doing in our garden in the middle of the night?"

"I don't know," Joe answered. "She didn't look like a burglar, did she? Perhaps she was staying here last week with her family and left something behind in the garden."

"No. We are the very first people to stay here, don't you remember? The house used to belong to an old man and it was sold to pay his nursing costs – he was allowed to stay in it for the rest of his life. Let's go and have another look. We might find something in daylight that we missed last night."

The children spent a good hour searching every part of the garden and orchard that they thought the mysterious woman might have visited, but they did not unearth any clues. They found what might have been part of a footprint in a flower bed, but it was too indistinct to be conclusive. They peered briefly inside the dilapidated summer house, but it was empty and very dirty. Cobwebs festooned the walls and, since neither of the children liked spiders, they did not venture inside.

Feeling rather dejected, they went back to the house for refreshment and sat gloomily in the lounge, gazing out into the garden. Suddenly, Joe leapt to his feet. "I've got it," he shouted. "Real policemen use dogs to sniff things out. Let's set Barney on the woman's trail. He's sure to find something."

"Police dogs need something to sniff first," Elena pointed out, "so that they know what scent they're looking for."

"Well, Barney's a really clever dog." Joe responded. "We'll just tell him what we want him to do and then he'll know."

Elena felt very doubtful about this, but in the absence of a better plan she agreed to give it a go.

Joe called Barney to him and carefully and slowly explained the situation. It certainly looked as if Barney was listening and paying attention to everything Joe said. He sat with his head cocked to one side, gazing at him with his large, intelligent brown eyes.

Once Joe was satisfied that he had told Barney everything there was to know, he called the dog out into the garden. Elena followed, feeling less than hopeful about the success of this venture.

Joe directed Barney to look around the garden with cries of "Seek, Barney, seek!"

Every time the dog stopped and looked expectantly at Joe, he repeated his cries with renewed effort.

Barney certainly didn't seem to mind the search. He sniffed under bushes, between shrubs and round flowers, but he didn't manage to find anything. Elena was just about to tell Joe that she was fed up with this activity and it was a total waste of time, when Barney came bounding up with something in his mouth. He deposited the object at Joe's feet and stood wagging his tail energetically.

"Good dog! Well done, Barney!" shouted Joe as he bent down to retrieve the object.

"Look, Elena," Joe called to her. "It's a purse." He opened it and looked inside. "There's not much money in here, just a photo of an old man. Wait, there's a name and an address here in case the purse is lost and found."

Elena peered over Joe's shoulder and read the small card he held in his hand: " 'Martha Rawlings. 10 Lower Street, Hemington'. That's the village we drove through to get here, where we stopped to ask for directions. Let's take the purse inside and get Mum or Dad to phone the police."

"No, I don't think we should do that yet," Joe told Elena. "The woman didn't look like a bad person and she might get into serious trouble for breaking into the garden. Let's go and check her out first and then decide whether or not to tell the police."

Chapter 3

The children went indoors and asked their mother if they could go out for a ride on their bikes. "We'd like to cycle to Hemington," said Elena. "It's supposed to have a very historic and interesting church."

If their mother was surprised at their sudden interest in ancient buildings, she didn't show it. She warned them to be careful and watch and listen out for any traffic on the roads. Supplied with drinks and snacks, the children wheeled their bikes down the drive and set off along the narrow, country lanes.

Hemington was about five miles away and Joe and Elena enjoyed the experience of cycling through green, leafy lanes with the warm sun on their faces. All was still and quiet, with just the occasional sound of bird-song or the drone of a passing insect. Colourful wild flowers enlivened the verges and everything smelt sweet and fresh.

It took them about 40 minutes to arrive at the village. Once they reached the centre – which boasted a pub, a shop and not much else – they dismounted and wheeled their bikes along as they searched for Lower Street. The village was quite small so it did not take long to find the location they were searching for. No. 10 was at the end of a small row of terraced cottages. Compared to its neighbours, it looked very shabby and run down.

"We need to find somewhere where we can hide and keep watch on the house," Joe told Elena.

Both children looked around them for a suitable place. It had to be somewhere that two cyclists might reasonably stop for a rest without arousing suspicion. "What about over there, under that tree?" suggested Elena, pointing to a large old oak that stood opposite and slightly to the left of the cottage.

"That's perfect," agreed Joe.

They wheeled their bikes across the road and propped them against the ancient tree.

"Just imagine all the things that this tree has seen since it was planted. It must be hundreds of years old," Elena remarked.

The children sat in the shade of the oak's branches and ate their snacks and chatted. They had been there for about an hour when the door of No. 10 opened and a woman stepped outside.

"Look, it's her," hissed Joe, nudging Elena with his elbow. "C'mon, quick."

Hastily packing away their drinks bottles and snacks, Joe and Elena picked up their bikes and followed the woman. She entered the door of the village shop. The children pretended to be looking at the items displayed in the window as they strained to overhear her conversation. Fortunately, the warm weather meant that the door was propped open to allow a flow of air to enter the shop, so the children could hear what the woman was saying to the shopkeeper.

"Mr Davis, I'm very sorry. I seem to have lost my purse. Could you let me have a small loaf, a tin of cat food and some milk and I'll pay you as soon as I can get to the bank in town?"

"Of course," Mr Davis answered the woman kindly. "Anything else? Are you sure that you are eating enough, Martha? You are beginning to look rather thin."

"Oh, I'm fine," the woman replied hastily, "and, yes, that's all, thank you." Placing the items in a shopping bag, the woman left the shop.

As she passed the children, they got a close look at her. She seemed to be in her fifties and had a sad and careworn face. Her coat was threadbare and her shoes old and scuffed. As she set off back to her house, Elena turned to Joe. "I'm going to give her back her purse. I don't know why she was in our garden, but I'm sure that she is a good person and she looks very poor."

She ran after the woman before Joe could stop her. "Mrs Rawlings, Mrs Rawlings!" she called.

Mrs Rawlings stopped and turned round. "Yes?" she asked. "Do I know you?"

"No," panted Elena. "We found your purse in a lane when we were out cycling and I just wanted to return it to you."

Mrs Rawlings looked at Elena quizzically as she held out her hand, as though she seemed to recognise her from somewhere. "Thank you. That's very kind and honest of you, even though there's not much money in it. Do you live in the village?"

"Oh no, we're just here on holiday," Elena replied.

By this time Joe had arrived on the scene. He saw that Mrs Rawlings was about to re-enter her house, and his investigative powers were not yet satisfied. "Excuse me," he said to her. "Could I please fill up my bottle with water? It's thirsty work cycling."

Mrs Rawlings hesitated as though she was about to refuse this request, but then said, "Of course, come with me." She led both children into the house. The inside was equally shabby to the outside, and rather empty. A large tabby cat emerged from one of the rooms to greet them. Elena bent down to stroke it.

"That's Monty," Mrs Rawlings told her. "He loves any fuss and attention." She led the children into a small, damp kitchen and took their bottles to the sink to fill. The kitchen window looked out on to stunning views of the surrounding hills.

"What a fantastic view!" said Elena. "You must love looking out of your window at that."

"Yes, I do," agreed Mrs Rawlings, "but I may not be able to enjoy it for much longer. I may have to move."

It seemed rude to question the woman about her personal affairs, so the children thanked her for the water and set off back to Southfield House. "Well, she seems like a very nice person," said Elena, "but something is wrong. She is sad and thin and she seems really poor."

"I agree," Joe responded, "but how can we find out what's wrong and why she was in our garden?"

Chapter 4

The children continued to discuss Mrs Rawlings as they cycled back to Southfield House. "Do you think that she'll come back to our garden again?" Elena asked Joe.

"Well, we interrupted her last time, so I bet that she didn't get what she was looking for," Joe replied. "I think she'll come back again."

"But what can we do?" Elena asked him. "We can't sit up and wait night after night until she returns."

"We'll have to set a trap," Joe said, though he wasn't sure quite what he meant by that.

Joe and Elena spent the rest of the day puzzling over plans. They had some brilliant ideas, but most of them were beyond their capabilities to put into practice. Eventually, they decided on simple trip-wires placed in strategic positions and attached to items in their bedrooms. Obviously, they had to set the traps just before they went to bed so that their parents didn't set them off during the day.

On the first evening they went to bed full of anticipation and were disappointed to wake up the following morning to find the traps still set. The same happened the next night. The children felt rather dejected as they set the traps on the third evening. "I think we must have frightened Mrs Rawlings off for good," said Elena.

"Maybe," answered Joe, "but let's keep going for a few more nights. You never know."

It was still dark when a bunch of keys jangled close by Joe's head. A trip had been set off. Instantly he was alert and leapt out of bed. Running past Elena's door, he called "Wake up! We're on!"

Racing down the stairs, he flew out of the back door without even stopping to put on any shoes. He knew exactly where the trip-wire was, so he did not have to search in the dark. As he moved quickly towards it, he saw a dim, dark shape struggling to stand upright on the path. "Stop!" shouted Joe. "Don't move."

The figure started to hobble down the path away from him, so Joe called again, "Mrs Rawlings, stop! I know it's you."

The figure came to a halt and turned to face him. In the hazy moonlight Joe saw the pale, anxious face of Mrs Rawlings. He walked up to her. "Don't be frightened," he told her. "I hope you haven't hurt yourself on the trip-wire. We needed a way to talk to you about why you are in our garden in the middle of the night."

Mrs Rawlings pulled up her coat to examine her knees. "Just a slight graze on the right one," she said. "Nothing to worry about. You're the boy who returned my purse with your sister, aren't you?" Joe nodded.

"Yes, I do owe you an explanation," Mrs Rawlings continued. "Perhaps we could sit down."

By this time Elena had joined the pair. She decided that cups of tea were needed all round and went to prepare these as Joe and Mrs Rawlings seated themselves on the garden chairs. When all three were settled with mugs of hot tea, Mrs Rawlings began.

"I grew up in this house, but I have lived abroad most of my adult life. My father was widowed when he was 80 and was in poor health by then. I decided to return to look after him, but I had to complete some work I was involved with and pack up my home abroad. That took several months. In the meantime, my father arranged some private nursing through an agency. His nurse seemed very kind and helpful, but even so my father deteriorated rapidly and became very muddled in his thinking. Anyway, to cut a long story short, when I did finally get back to this country I discovered that the nurse was a very wicked woman indeed. She had given my father drugs to make him confused. He had sold his home and she had taken all the money and anything of value from the house and disappeared. By this time, my father was very ill. His little dog, Poppy, had died and, having nothing else to live for, his health had declined rapidly. Before he died, he just managed to tell me that he had hidden a very valuable diamond ring in Poppy's collar, which he buried with her ashes. He was worried that the evil nurse would find the ring. He had left me a clue to the whereabouts of the grave, but he died before he could tell me the clue. Although I searched, I could not find the grave and I had to leave the house soon after as the new owner wanted to use it as a holiday home. I gathered up my father's few remaining possessions and left.

"My own circumstances, as you saw, are not good. I haven't been able to find work and I fear that I will soon lose my home as my money is fast running out. I was sorting through my father's old papers and I found something I hadn't noticed before. I think it could be the clue to the whereabouts of Poppy's grave. The trouble is that I can't work it out. I thought that if I came to the garden I might see something that would help me make sense of the clue, but you interrupted my first attempt and tonight has ended equally badly."

As she finished her story, a tear slowly trickled down Mrs Rawlings' cheek.

Chapter 5

Both children were very touched by Mrs Rawlings' sad story. "Perhaps we could help you search," suggested Elena.

"Yes," added Joe, "we could all look at the clue together. Three brains are better than one."

Mrs Rawlings handed them a piece of paper. At a glance, the children could see that a short poem was written on the paper. It wasn't the sort of clue that Joe had been imagining at all.

" 'For Martha Hari'," read Elena.

"Who's that?" Joe asked.

"Oh," laughed Mrs Rawlings, "that was my father's nick-name for me. There was a very famous female spy called Mata Hari. When I was a child, I was always playing spy games with my friends, so my father dubbed me Martha Hari. I expect he used that title on the poem because only I would know who it was meant for. Anyone else looking at this would think he had misspelt the name."

Elena continued to read from the paper:

> *Our beautiful red flower has faded and now it is gone to a distant place.*
> *Here myriad grains are marked with pinks and whites as delicate as lace*
> *And Jolly Jack sings a shanty with a weather-beaten face.*

"What on earth does that mean," said Joe, "and what's 'myriad'?"

"Myriad means many, many – you know, thousands and thousands," explained Mrs Rawlings. "The red flower fading refers to Poppy dying and I think that 'myriad' means the grains of sand on a beach."

"And Jolly Jack is a sailor and a shanty is a sea-song," Joe said excitedly. "The place must have some connection with the sea. I'll go and get a torch, then we can look around together. Maybe there is something to do with a boat in the garden."

Armed with a pair of torches to light their way, all three began a systematic search of the garden and orchard. They looked in every nook and cranny, up high and down low, but there didn't seem to be anything that had a connection with the sea. After some considerable time, they gathered on the patio disconsolately.

"Well, we've looked everywhere and there's absolutely nothing," grumbled Joe.

"There is one area we haven't searched yet," said Mrs Rawlings. "The small garden beyond the arch, but I don't think that it is a likely place. Still, come on, we'd better take a look."

The three walked together into the small circular garden, but there was plainly nothing boat-like in there. They were turning to leave when Elena suddenly shouted, "Wait! I know where it is. On the day that we arrived I came in here and saw a beautiful shell pattern on the ground. Don't you see, shells are from the beach? They are delicate, pink and white and perhaps they mark the spot where the collar is buried. I picked up some shells to show my mother and meant to put them back again, but I forgot."

"I think she could be right," agreed Mrs Rawlings. "Can you remember where they were?"

"Over here," said Elena, leading the others to the plot in the gravelled area.

"I'll go and find something to dig with," said Joe, running off.

He was soon back with a spade, and began to dig furiously while Elena and Mrs Rawlings waited with bated breath. Slowly a circular, muddy shape began to emerge. Joe bent down and picked it up, giving it a vigorous shake as he straightened up. Particles of mud flew off to reveal a red, leather dog's collar.

"Hurrah!" shouted Elena. "We've found it."

"But is the diamond ring inside it?" asked Mrs Rawlings.

Joe pulled at the collar. The stitching had rotted in the damp earth and it easily pulled apart. Something shiny fell to the ground. "Yes, here it is," said Joe and placed it gently in Mrs Rawlings' hands.

The three examined the ring together. It contained a very large diamond. "This will be worth a lot of money," Mrs Rawlings told the children. "If I sell it I will be able to keep my home and do the necessary repairs to it. I don't know how to thank you for your help."

"Perhaps we could come to tea with you before we leave," suggested Elena. "There is one thing I'd like to know, though. On the first night that we saw you, you seemed to vanish into thin air. I thought you were a ghost. How did you do that?"

Mrs Rawlings grinned at her. "Come with me," she said, "and all will be revealed."

She led Elena and Joe down the garden and into the orchard. Arriving at the summer house, Mrs Rawlings pushed open the door and went inside. Joe and Elena shined their torches after her.

"I told you that my friends and I used to play spies. Well, we had a secret, hidden door at the back of the summer house." Mrs Rawlings pressed on two of the wooden panels and they opened to reveal a hedge behind. There was a gap in the hedge large enough for a person to squeeze through into the field beyond. "So now you know my secret," she grinned.

Joe and Elena smiled back. "We're so happy that everything has turned out well in the end," said Elena. "We never thought that we would have such an amazing adventure on our holiday, though."

And they all laughed.

Follow-up work for each chapter

CHAPTER 1

In pairs, ask the children to draw a design of and label or write about their ideal garden. Tell them to think of all the items they would include and why – for example, for their attractive appearance, for fun, for comfort, for plants or animals.

CHAPTER 2

Ask the children either to write their own story or to draw a comic strip about a ghost in a haunted house. Ask them to think about why the ghost is haunting the house. Do they become involved in an exciting adventure?

CHAPTER 3

Use the Spy jacket template, 1.1 (p. 24), copied on A3 paper. (The broken lines on the template indicate fold lines.) Ask the children to design a jacket with all sorts of spy gadgets inside and out and write a description of the ways in which they would be the perfect spy.

CHAPTER 4

Put the children into small groups. Ask them to choose one of these three scenarios and devise a trap. They must act out what would happen:

1   You work in a castle. You have heard that a burglar is planning to break in to steal a silver plate.

2   You think an alien is living in your garden shed, but every time you try to surprise it, it hides.

3   You want to catch a beautiful wild stallion, but it is very quick and you can't get near it.

CHAPTER 5

Ask the children to write or draw about digging up something special. What might it be – treasure, something magical, a lost artefact? When they have finished, tell them to describe their article to a friend and say what they would do with it.

Ideas for maths work

Surveys

Put the children into mixed-ability pairs. Ask them to devise a survey for the rest of the class to complete relating to gardens. For example, they might choose eight vegetables, fruit or garden animals and ask everyone to choose their favourite. They can record the answers as a tally chart, then make a bar chart of their results.

Estimate and measure

Choose some distances outside. Ask the children to estimate, then measure, them in footsteps and metres. Alternatively, you could ask the children to estimate, then weigh, a selection of vegetables.

The incredible adventure of number

Using their own copy of The incredible adventure of number template, 1.2 (p. 25), copied on A3 paper, each child works on the journey of a number through a garden. They are to prepare their sheet for another child to complete. They should fill in the large boxes with writing or drawings describing or showing the events they choose to happen during the journey. Each time something bad happens on the journey a number they choose and write in the small box (inside each large box) is subtracted (e.g. a bird tries to eat you: –2; a dog chases you: –4). When an addition sign is indicated, something good happens (e.g. you find a delicious strawberry to eat: +3; you cool off in the pond: +6). The children must calculate the total as they go, to avoid getting into minus numbers. They need to keep their running total on a piece of scrap paper. If appropriate, tell them to adjust the activity, for instance including large numbers or multiplication and division (only with exact answers) or even fractions. Once they have completed their sheet and worked out their calculations, they give their journey to a friend, who writes their calculations in the boxes. At the end, they check to see if they have both arrived at the same number. If not, they work through the journey together again to see why.

Coordinates

Plot the following coordinates on squared paper to create a character from the story and their house. Write the character's name on the house.

Create a grid with the letters A–T along the bottom and the numbers 0–17 up the side. First, join the coordinates to make the house:

(C,6) (A,6) (A,12) (E,17) (I,12) (I,6) (G,6) (G,11) (C,11) (C,6) (G,6)

Now join the coordinates to make the character:

(L,5) (L,6) (M,6) (M,11) (J,11) (J,13) (L,14) (M,14) (N,15) (N,12) (R,12) (R,14) (S,15) (S,5) (Q,5) (Q,6) (R,6) (R,9) (N,9) (N,5) (L,5)

Number quiz

Put the children into mixed-ability pairs and ask them to devise a number quiz to be completed outside. For example, they might ask questions like these:

- How many [e.g. fence posts] are there?
- What is the length of ... in metres?
- How many rectangles can they see when you face ... [building]?
- Put [named items] in order of shortest to tallest.

Before they do this, talk through the maths operations they could include, so that they can make suggestions and provide plenty of ideas. Once the quizzes have been written, the children can swap sheets and complete another pair's quiz.

Science activities

Find a warm bed for little mouse

In this investigation, the children compare beds of different materials to find the warmest. For example, leaves, paper, straw or sand could be used for bedding and placed in a box or plastic bag. Depending on the availability of resources, the children do this in groups of 6 to 8, or you demonstrate it with assistance from them in collecting the bedding and packing the beds. Place identical bottles of hot water into the centre of each bed. Record the water temperature at the beginning of the experiment and again at the end to see which bottle is the warmest (i.e. has lost the least heat). Before the experiment begins the children could guess which bed they think will be the warmest. Encourage them to discuss their findings about how the materials compared with regard to preventing the loss of heat.

Vegetable tasting

Chop up a selection of fruit and vegetables (e.g. onions, carrots, apples, celery, grapes, cabbage). Ask the children to wear blindfolds. Get them to taste the samples to see if they can guess what each is. Record their results. Repeat the experiment, but this time ask the children to wear the blindfold and hold their noses tightly as well. Discuss whether the second set of results is different from the first? Explain that we can distinguish only a few different tastes, but thousands of smells.

Other activities

Team quiz

Put the children into two mixed-ability teams. The questions are designed so that every child should be able to answer at least one question. For each question choose two children, one from each team, using your knowledge of them to pair children of similar ability. The first child to answer correctly wins a point for their team.

1   What is a marigold?

2   Fill in the missing stage frogspawn ... frog.

3   Name an insect with a red back with black spots on it.

4   Name a vegetable beginning with C.

5   What is a perennial?

6   What are secateurs used for?

7   What is a thrush?

8   Spell 'hydrangea'.

9   Fill in the missing stage caterpillar ... butterfly.

10   How many legs does an insect have?

11   How many letters are repeated in 'wheelbarrow'?

12   Arrange these letters into a garden animal: 'rdipes'.

13   What is the fruit of an oak tree called?

14   What is a deciduous tree?

15   What bird has a red breast?

16   Name the four seasons.

17   What is the name of a structure in which plants are kept warm?

18   Name a garden animal that hibernates.

19   Spell 'trowel'.

20   Name a herb used in cooking.

What am I?

Cut out the garden cards on template 1.3 (p. 26). The children take turns to have a card attached to their back. They turn round so that the rest of the class can see their illustration, then ask questions until they discover what they are. It might be a good idea to show the children all the cards before playing so that they know what's involved. You could ask the children to make additional cards with different items.

Garden word search

Use the garden world search template, 1.4 (p. 27). The instructions are on the worksheet.

A garden message

Give each child a copy of template 1.5 (p. 28). Ask the children to work out the message.

Follow the clues

The clues are on template 1.6, and they relate to the scene on template 1.7 (pp. 29 and 30). Give each child their own copies.

Active games

All change in the garden

The children sit in a circle. Label them 'Ant', 'Spider' and 'Ladybird' consecutively around the circle. When you call out one or more of these categories, the children with those labels swap seats. If you call 'Garden', they all change. To make the game more exciting, have one fewer chair than there are children. The child who is without a chair must try to obtain one while a changeover is taking place.

Carrots and swedes

The children stand in a circle facing inwards. The game is played like Duck, duck, goose. One child begins the action by walking round the outside of the circle. They tap each child gently on the shoulder as they pass behind and say 'Carrot' or 'Swede'. If they say 'Swede', the child touched leaves the circle and runs in the opposite direction to the tapper. The object of the game is to try to be first back to the space left in the circle by the 'Swede'. The game continues with a new tapper.

The bean game

The children find a space to stand in. Explain that you will call out different categories of bean. Each bean has a different action that the children must perform:

- Runner bean – run on the spot
- Broad bean – stretch out arms and legs like a star
- French bean – crouch down and bunny-jump
- String bean – stand on tip-toe and stretch arms above head
- Jumping bean – jump on the spot
- Jelly bean – shake arms and legs
- African bean – turn quickly in circles.

Go through the list of beans and get the children to practise the relevant actions. Explain to them that when they become tired they may stop. Call out the categories, speeding up as you go, to see who will be the last person to join in each time. While the game is new to the children, you can demonstrate each action as you call it out.

The giant's garden

Prior to playing the game, ask the children each to make and colour a flower, approximately A5 size. The children sit or stand in a circle. One child is chosen to be the giant and kneels in the centre of the circle wearing a blindfold. The flowers are scattered on the floor around the kneeling giant. Choose two children, who have to enter the circle and try to collect as many flowers as they can. The giant must listen for any sounds they make and tag them. If a child is tagged, they must return to their place in the circle with the flowers they have collected. The game ends either when both children have been tagged or all the flowers have been collected. The children count the flowers to see who has collected the most.

Vegetable relay

You can use drawn, plastic or real vegetables for this game. The children are put into four teams at one end of the room. Their selection of vegetables, an equal number for each team, is placed at the other end of the room. Each team has a 'vegetable pot'. On the command 'Go', the first member of each team runs to the other end of the room, collects a vegetable and returns. When the vegetable has been placed in the pot, the next member of the team sets off. The winning team is the first to have all their vegetables in the pot and be seated.

Art

Decorate a dog competition

Using template 1.8, Hiding Barney (p. 31), the children decorate the dog for a competition. They could, for example,, use scraps of fabric in a collage or create a fantasy dog that is multi-coloured. Encourage them to use their imagination to create something interesting.

Three-dimensional flowers

Create three-dimensional flowers, using template 1.9 (p. 32) enlarged and copied on to stiff card. These are particularly effective if the flowers are decorated with small pieces of scrunched-up tissue paper or small squares of a bright fabric.

Clay bugs

Using quick-drying clay, make and paint garden bugs. Arrange them on a table top decorated to resemble a garden.

Butterflies

Using the butterfly on template 1.9 (p. 32), the children can make one of two options.

1   The butterfly can be cut from black sugar paper. The children cut shapes out of the wings and cover the holes that are created with coloured tissue paper to give a stained-glass window effect.

2   The butterfly is cut from white paper. A blob of paint is applied to one wing, one colour at a time. After each application, the butterfly is folded in half with the painted section inside and pressure is applied to the wings. This spreads the paint in a symmetrical pattern on both wings. The butterfly is opened out and a different colour is then applied to another part of the wing.

Egg-box spiders

Spiders may be made from the raised sections of a cardboard egg-box. These are cut out and painted black. Attach black pipe-cleaners (or you can paint white pipe-cleaners black) as legs. Out of string, the children could make a giant web on which to place their spiders.

Spy jacket

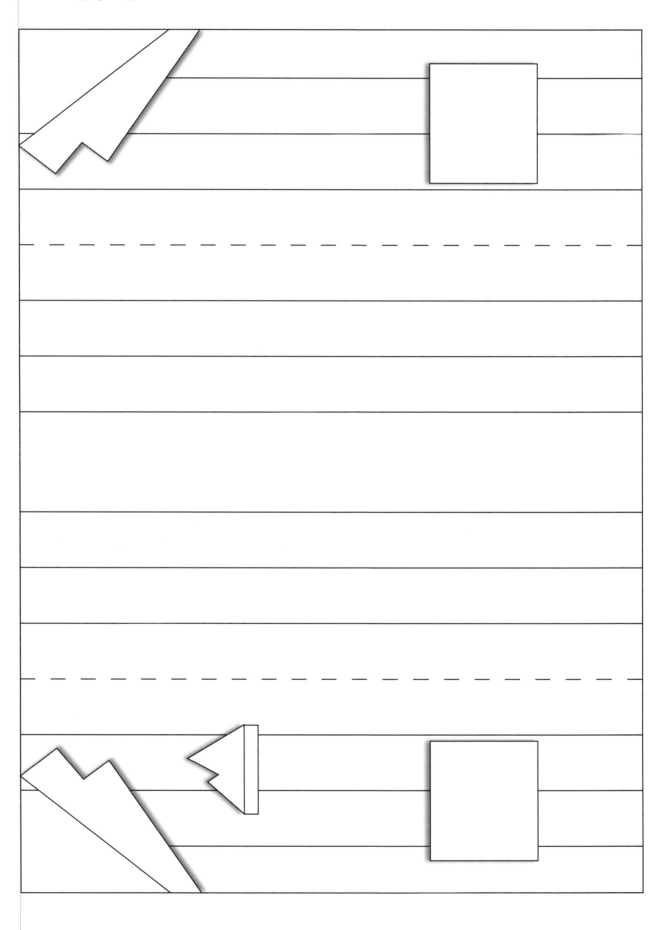

1.2

The incredible adventure of number

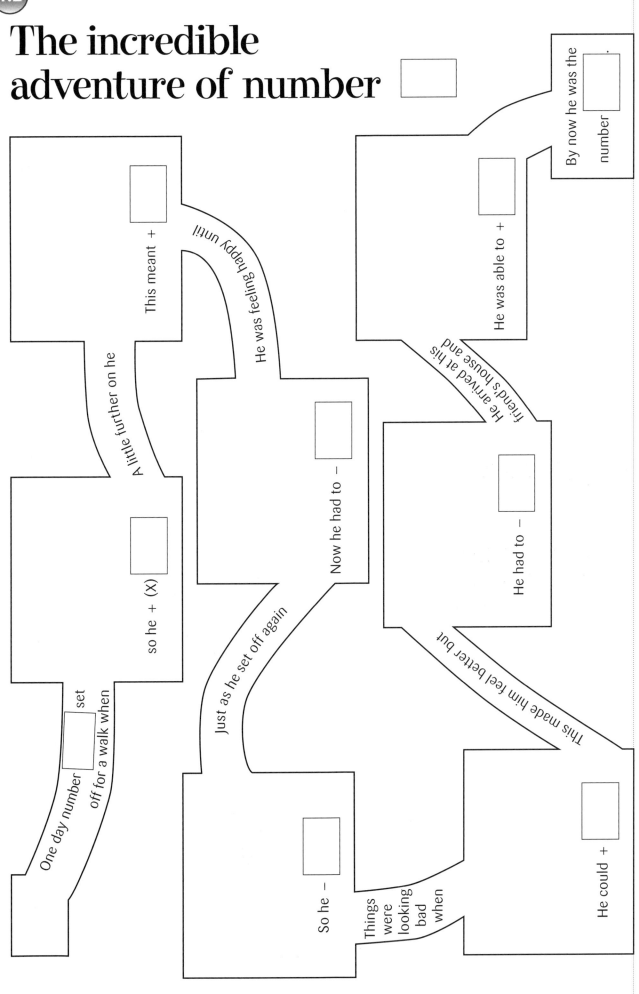

This meant +

A little further on he

He was feeling happy until

By now he was the number   .

He was able to +

He arrived at his friend's house and

so he + (X)

Now he had to –

He had to –

Just as he set off again

This made him feel better but

One day number   set off for a walk when

So he –

Things were looking bad when

He could +

1.3

What am I?

greenhouse

carrot

worm

flower pot

trowel

spade

bird

watering can

ladybird

nest

wheelbarrow

shed

deckchair

flower

spider

lawnmower

Garden word search

S	P	A	L	T	B	U	G	O	M	A	K
W	T	R	O	W	E	L	P	R	A	W	C
I	O	F	E	N	C	E	O	S	A	A	I
N	W	A	L	L	A	W	N	T	F	S	T
G	L	A	D	Y	B	I	R	D	S	P	S
S	E	E	D	G	R	E	E	N	T	E	R
A	A	E	U	F	L	D	M	O	I	S	E
P	F	E	B	L	A	C	K	B	I	R	D
P	A	R	U	P	F	L	O	W	E	R	I
L	O	T	S	T	O	N	E	W	A	P	P
E	O	S	H	E	R	B	O	R	A	S	S
P	O	G	S	T	A	M	O	U	S	E	L

Find the words listed below. Words read horizontally from left to right, vertically and diagonally up or down. Some letters are used in more than one word.

SPADE	TREE	PATH	TROWEL	WORM
GRASS	FENCE	APPLE	BLACKBIRD	MOWER
BUG	FLY	STICK	HERB	LOG
FLOWER	BUD	LEAF	SEED	LADYBIRD
BUSH	GREEN	LAWN	MOUSE	STONE
POT	WASP	SPIDER	WALL	SWING

A garden message

A = !	B = "	C = £	D = $	E = %
F = ^	G = &	H = *	I = (	J =)
K = +	L = {	M = }	N = [	O =]
P = :	Q = @	R = #	S = ~	T = <
U = >	V = ?	W = /	X = \	Y = |
Z = X				

Work out the message below and write your answer in the same code.

/*!<   (~ |]># ^!?]>#(<%   <*([&   ([!   &!#$%[

Now answer this question

/*!<   (~   "(&&%#   !   }]>~%   ]#   ![![<

Make up a code of your own with a partner and send a message to each other.

Follow the clues

Look on the illustration to find the number of the next clue on your clue sheet.
Cross off the numbers once you have visited them. At the end, unscramble
the letters in the boxes to make a garden word.

Start: Look for somewhere you can sit and relax to enjoy the view of the garden (go to no. **4**).

1 There's plenty of food on the bird table. If you were hungry, you might like some of these orange-coloured vegetables.

2 Once you've had a cool off in the pool, look for something you might use to help you shift leaves in the autumn.

3 Birds like to nest on a branch. Now look for something that you could use to give the plants a drink.

4 Once you've had a rest, find something that is made of panels and started life as a tree.

5 When you have your huge marrow, you might want to plant some seeds in one of these.

6 There's two of this letter in 'carrots', but you only want one for your box. Then find something tall you might like to climb.

7 The runner bean urges you to race to somewhere you can cool off on a hot day.

8 A spade is very handy when you want to dig up some vegetables. You may want one of these large green ones for lunch.

9 Take the round letter from your pots to put in your box, then see if you can find somewhere for a bird to live.

10 Sheds are useful places for all your garden tools, but you need to look for something that likes to eat flies.

11 Take the tall, thin letter and put it in your box, then move on to somewhere you could be high or low.

12 You can put the first letter of this in your box, then find somewhere to keep your garden tools.

13 Hurrah, you've reached the end! Draw the object from your box in the greenhouse, then colour the picture.

14 Put the second letter from this in your box, then find the sprinter in the vegetable patch.

15 Have some fun on the swing, then see if you can find some swimmers.

16 This big old tree wants to know if someone has caught any fish for tea.

17 The fish in the pond look healthy; now see if your feathered friends have plenty to eat.

18 The garden gnome hasn't had much luck with his rod. He sends you back to the vegetable patch to do some digging. Look for what you will need for this job.

19 Take the first letter for your box, then look for a bed where no one is sleeping, but beautiful things grow.

20 The plants here may help you unscramble the letters. Then go to somewhere with a colour in its name, even though it is made of glass.

Follow the clues picture

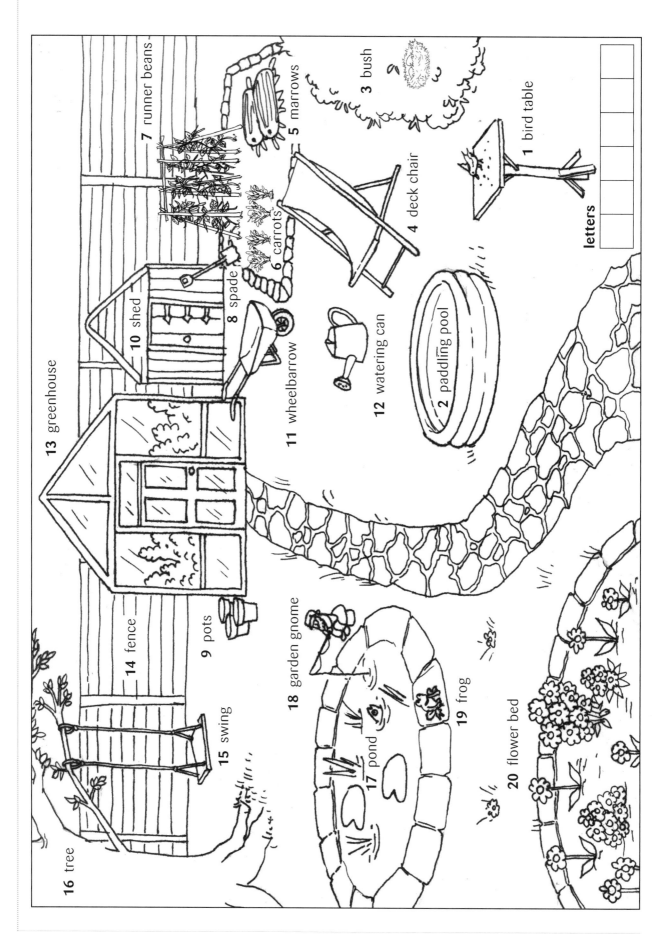

1.8

Hiding Barney

Templates for artwork

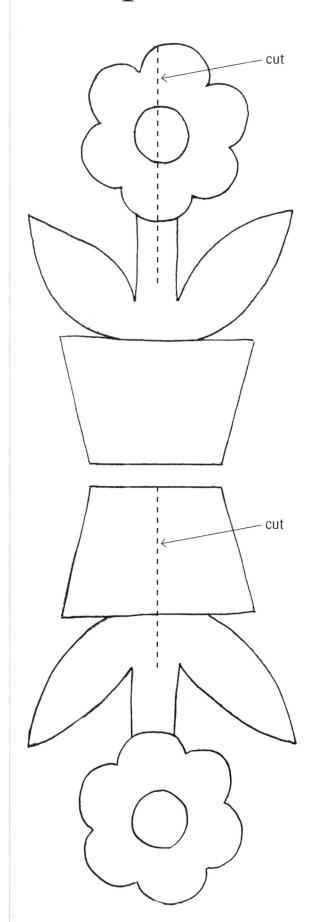

cut

cut

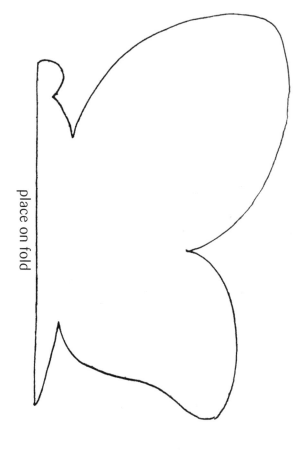

place on fold

Alfie in Space

The adventures of a space-travelling dog

Chapter 1

Space Exploration Incorporated was the largest of the space-discovery companies and Chuck Hampton was its most recently qualified astronaut. He and his partner, Bill Weatherby, a veteran of dozens of missions, had visited numerous planets and far-flung galaxies over the four years they had worked together. Most of the places they had visited were uninhabited and they were simply looking for the possibility of mining minerals or metal ores. Occasionally they found different life forms, but they were very basic and of little interest to the pair. The two astronauts enjoyed each other's company – which was just as well as they sometimes spent months away from Earth and family and friends, with just one another to talk to.

One day Chuck went into work and was called into the office of his boss, Harry Nailer. "'fraid I've some bad news for you, Chuck," he said. "Bill was taken ill over the weekend. He has to have a serious operation and is going to be out of action for some time. We're so short staffed at present that I can't find anyone to take his place while he's off. You're going to have to travel alone. I know that you're not as experienced as Bill, but I think you're ready to fly solo. Sorry to be giving you this bad news."

"I'm real sorry to hear about Bill," Chuck said, "but I'm sure I'll manage. I've had enough experience, I think, to know what I'm doing."

Chuck flew a couple of solo missions, but he felt very lonely on his own. One evening Chuck was at home between jobs. He was relaxing in his chair with a beer, watching the TV and stroking his dog's ears, when a sudden thought struck him. "Heck, Alfie," he said to his dog. "Why don't I take you with me on my missions? You're great company and I wouldn't feel so alone any more."

The following morning Chuck went to see Harry Nailer. "Boss," he began, "I'd like to take my dog Alfie with me in my ship while Bill's off sick. He's a real good mutt and he'd be helpful as well as keeping me company. He could carry things and fetch stuff for me, sniff out anything important and do all sorts of small but useful jobs."

At first, Harry was totally against the idea. "It's against regulations to take pets on missions," he told Chuck.

However, after half an hour of talk, Chuck had persuaded Harry that Alfie wasn't a pet, but a useful member of society and had wrung an agreement out of him. "The consequences are on your head though, Chuck. I'm taking no responsibility for anything that might happen with a dog on board. And you'll have to put him through all the checks to make sure that he can cope with conditions on board."

With just a week to go before his next mission, Chuck had no time to waste. He put Alfie through his paces and tested the dog's reactions to all sorts of conditions in a simulated spaceship. To give the dog his due, he came out with flying colours. He had fast responses and no adverse reactions. Chuck had a special space helmet made for Alfie, but after consultation with the experts, he decided that he didn't need a space suit as well.

The laboratory came up with specially formulated dog food that was suitable for conditions in the spaceship, and within the week everything was prepared for Alfie to travel with his master.

On the day of the mission Chuck was up at the crack of dawn to prepare all his and Alfie's equipment. He felt happier than he had been in months, since the onset of Bill's illness. He would no longer have to travel alone. He would at least be able to enjoy the companionship of his faithful dog.

On arriving at the compound, man and dog were fitted out in their space gear and walked to the waiting rocket. Alfie needed a bit of help to clamber up the steps, but soon enough both were strapped into their seats ready for take-off.

The rocket launchers were ignited and the count down began: "Ten, nine, eight, seven …"

"You ready, boy?" asked Chuck. Alfie wagged his tail.

"six, five, four, three, two …"

"Take it steady now, easy boy," soothed Chuck.

"one. BLAST OFF!"

The rocket whooshed up into the air. Alfie look somewhat panicked, but he remained still in his chair, and as the rocket soared ever higher he began to relax.

Once they had travelled through Earth's atmosphere and were safely beyond, Chuck unbuckled himself first and then Alfie. "Well then. boy," he said. "Welcome to space and your first mission."

Chapter 2

Over the next few days the ship travelled through space at an incredible speed on its way to a distant planet. Alfie looked out through the port-hole at the amazing views of stars and galaxies and the beautiful swirling colours in the pitch-black sky.

Man and dog settled into a routine aboard the spaceship. With the company of Alfie, the days did not seem so long and tedious to Chuck. He chatted away, pointing out landmarks and items of interest on their journey. Even though Alfie could not talk back to his master, he seemed to appreciate the travelogue and looked eagerly at everything that Chuck indicated to him.

On the sixth day they reached their destination. This was a small planet that Chuck and Bill had visited some years earlier to install a mining device that extracted a rare and precious ore. Part of the device had started to malfunction and Chuck had brought along a replacement part with which to repair the machine.

He spoke to Alfie as he dressed himself in his suit and helmet for outside work. "Well, Alfie. This will be your first taste of life outside Earth. Not much to see here though, boy. A few weird plants, but no intelligent life."

Once Chuck and Alfie were suitably attired, the astronaut opened the hatch and they descended from the spaceship to the ground below. The surface was hard underfoot, with a dusting of a silvery, grey powder. The landscape was very flat and uninteresting with the occasional spindly looking plant dotted here and there at infrequent intervals.

Alfie wandered over to one of the plants and sniffed at it. Its branches were thin and brittle looking, with a scattering of small, coarse leaves. Alfie lifted his leg, as dogs do to mark territory, when a thought popped into his head. "Excuse me, do you mind!"

Alfie jumped and looked around him. There was nothing and nobody there. He turned back and saw that the plant was shaking itself vigorously. Another thought entered his head. "Just what do you think you are doing, contaminating my leaves?"

Alfie took a step back and barked at the plant. "And don't shout at me either" was the next thing that he thought.

Alfie was puzzled. "What on earth is going on?" he thought.

This was immediately answered by another thought. "I'm communicating with you, of course."

"Is that plant putting thoughts into my head?" thought Alfie, "or am I going mad?"

"No, you're not going mad. It is I, the plant. I'm practising thought transference with you and I can read what you're thinking as well."

"Well, dang me," thought Alfie. "I've never met a plant that could communicate with me before."

"And I've never seen a furry thing like you before," responded the plant.

"Can you communicate with Chuck as well?" thought Alfie.

"Is Chuck that two-legged silver creature who arrived with you?" the plant asked.

"Yes," thought Alfie.

"Oh, we can read his thoughts, but he can't tune in to ours. He's obviously a much more primitive life form than you are."

Alfie was very amused by this. He wished that he could inform Chuck of the plant's impression of him. It would be really funny to see Chuck's face when he told him that the plant considered the dog to be a more intelligent species than the human being.

"Are there other life forms on the planet?" thought Alfie.

"No, just us plants," came the response. "We're very happy here. We have everything we need and our thoughts are so strong that we can communicate with one another, however distant we are from each other. We spend our days having great conversations and telling each other jokes. It's a great life."

Just then Chuck returned, having completed his repair. "Time to go, boy," he said to Alfie, then, "Why are you staring at that plant so intently? It won't bite you." He laughed at his own humour.

"You see what I mean about the silver two-legged creature being stupid?" queried the plant.

"Oh yes, I do indeed," thought Alfie.

He followed Chuck up into the spaceship. As he closed the hatch, Chuck said,

"A bit boring that place, eh, boy? Just a few straggly plants, no intelligent life forms there."

Alfie shook his head in mock despair, closed his eyes and went to sleep.

Chapter 3

Alfie's next opportunity for space exploration came several weeks later, when Chuck was asked to visit a recently discovered planet. As far as anyone knew, it hadn't been visited by humans before and Chuck was very excited to be the first man to set foot there.

"Imagine," he said to Alfie. "If there are any life forms there, they will have never seen a human or a dog before. They might be a bit wary of you, a great, hairy, dumb mutt, but I'll be there to protect you, boy."

Alfie looked up at his master and wagged his tail.

The new planet had been named Stalia, and the pair of intrepid space explorers arrived after two weeks aboard their spaceship. Having disembarked, they stood for a minute to look at their new surroundings. This planet was certainly more interesting than the previous one. There seemed to be a great variety of plants, flowering shrubs and trees of many different hues. There was no sign, however, of any building or human-like life form.

"Now then, Alfie," Chuck said, "I want you to wait here while I go ahead and scout the terrain. I want to make sure that there is no potential danger for you. OK, boy. Now SIT, good boy, and STAY!"

Patiently, Alfie did as he was bid. He lay down and watched as his master disappeared into the thick vegetation. "I hope he's safe on his own out there," he thought.

He was just starting to become a little bored when he heard a deep growl. Looking in the direction of the sound, he saw something waving from a hole in the ground. On closer inspection, it appeared to be a hairy hand. Alfie leapt, bounded over and peered intently into the hole. He was greeted by a large furry face staring up at him.

"How d'you do," the thing growled at Alfie. It wasn't human talk, but the growling was very dog-like, so Alfie had no problem understanding it.

"Oh, I'm fine," Alfie replied in his best growl. "I'm called Alfie. What's your name?"

"Toosha," was the growled reply. "What are you doing here? And that great, dumb-looking silver mutt, is that your pet?"

"Erm, we've just discovered your planet, on Earth, and so we thought we would come along and take a look. And yes, that's my pet out there. He's kinda stupid, but loyal. I just let him go for a little walk to get some exercise," growled Alfie.

"I hope he's all right out there by himself. The vegetation around here isn't too friendly. Well, come inside. We're just about to eat so you can join us for dinner." Toosha disappeared down the hole and Alfie followed. This, of course, was easy for a dog. Alfie grinned to himself as he thought of the struggle Chuck would have had following them down the underground passage.

The passage opened into a large room. It was full of furry creatures like Toosha, and they were all seated around a long table that was laden with delicious-looking food. Alfie's mouth began to water and he wiped away the dribble with his paw. After being introduced to all the furry inhabitants, Alfie joined them at the table. They tucked into the food, which proved to be just as tasty as it looked.

Suddenly a loud, piercing sound filled the air. "Tree alert! Tree alert!" growled Alfie's neighbour, leaping up from the table. All the other diners followed suit.

"North-west sector," growled one of the furry creatures, and they all dashed down a passage behind Alfie's chair that led out of the room.

"What's going on?" Alfie inquired of Toosha as he charged past.

"A tree's caught something," Toosha growled. "Remember I told you the vegetation was unfriendly round here? That's why we live underground. Sometimes we have to go up, though, and the trees try to catch us and squeeze us to death. We devised a warning system that lets us know if something gets caught and its whereabouts. We can attack the tree roots from underground and usually manage a rescue. Sometimes we're too late, though."

Toosha raced ahead and Alfie bounded after him. He had a very anxious, queasy, feeling in the pit of his stomach, and a few minutes later his worst fears were confirmed.

When he arrived at the source of the warning sound, a viewing tube showed quite plainly that Chuck was held fast in the branches of a huge tree.

"Oh, that's my pet," Alfie growled to the furry creatures. "Please, please, can you save him?"

At once they set upon the roots of the tree that dangled into their underground passage. They bit and clawed the roots ferociously while Alfie continued to watch through the viewing tube. Chuck's face was growing more and more purple and his frantic struggling was becoming weaker and weaker. After what seemed like an eternity, but was probably only several minutes, the combined efforts of the furry creatures had the desired effect. The branches of the tree suddenly flew apart and Chuck slithered to the ground, where he lay panting.

"I must go and help him," Alfie growled, and the furry creatures led him to an opening nearby. Before he crawled out, Alfie thanked them for their hospitality and bade them goodbye.

"Be careful," warned Toosha. "Keep away from the trees."

Alfie scrabbled out of the hole and went up to his master. He nudged Chuck again and again with his nose until the recovering astronaut looked up.

"Well, hello there, Alfie," he gasped. "Boy, am I glad to see you. I think my suit must have got caught up in the branches of that tree. I had a real struggle to get free."

Later on, when they were safely back on the spaceship and Chuck had fully recovered, he prepared their evening meal. "Dinner time," he called to Alfie.

Alfie, who was still full up from the enormous feast he had enjoyed earlier, just opened an eye then closed it again.

"What's up, boy? You off your food? Poor Alfie, you must be feeling under the weather." Chuck patted the dog's head.

"If you only knew the truth," thought Alfie, then fell into a deep sleep and dreamt about little furry creatures.

Chapter 4

"We're off to planet Fargion tomorrow," Chuck told Alfie some weeks later. "Scientists believe that there are human-like life forms there and I'm going to try to make contact with them."

"That should be entertaining," Alfie thought to himself, but he just wagged his tail and looked pleased for Chuck.

Their first glimpse of Fargion, when they arrived, certainly looked promising. A variety of buildings were plainly visible and they could also see what looked like forms of transport. "Come on then, Alfie," called Chuck once they were suitably attired. "Let's mosey along into town and see what there is to see."

No sooner had they entered what appeared to be the main street of the town, than they were surrounded by a large group of excited inhabitants. They had a definite similarity to humans, being two legged and upright, although their appearance was very different. They wore no clothes as their entire bodies were covered in folds of what looked like soft purple leather. Their faces seemed friendly, though, which was encouraging.

Chuck tried out a greeting. "Hello. My name's Chuck and I bring you greetings from planet Earth."

The group of inhabitants looked at him blankly. Chuck tried various different languages to no avail. He then thought of trying to sign his message. Pointing to himself, he said, "Me Chuck." He followed this with a detailed display of hand signals as he tried to convey the information that he had travelled from Earth in a spaceship to make contact with the people of Fargion.

Close to Alfie, one of the aliens turned to his neighbour and began to communicate in a high-pitched whistle. "Why's that Earthling waving his arms around like a windmill? Is he mad?"

Alfie realised that although he could understand the aliens, their whistles were outside of the range of human hearing. Turning to the alien who had spoken he barked a response.

"Did you understand what I said?" whistled the alien, looking down at Alfie in astonishment.

Alfie barked an affirmative.

"We know all about planet Earth," whistled the aliens. "We were hoping never to have any visitors from there as humans seem rather stupid creatures. I can see now that our opinion was correct. I think we'll leave him to wander around on his own for a while and then hopefully he'll just go away."

"Please, is there any way you can communicate with him?" barked Alfie. "He will have a hard time from his boss if he goes home without having made proper contact with you. He may seem stupid, but he's very kind."

"Well, you seem intelligent, and since you ask so politely we'll do it for you. We can't speak as we don't have vocal cords, but we can download all the information in the Earthling's brain and then read and write his language."

The alien stepped up to Chuck and held out a hand in greeting. When the astronaut responded, the alien held his hand, closed his eyes and concentrated for several seconds. Releasing Chuck's hand, he whistled for someone to fetch something from a building nearby.

In five minutes he was handed a piece of equipment, similar in appearance to a lap-top computer. Placing a finger on the screen, the alien thought and a message appeared on the screen instantly – and in English.

Chuck and Alfie read, "Greetings, Earthling. We are pleased to welcome you to the planet Fargion. I cannot speak to you, but if you talk to me, I can reply in writing on the screen."

Chuck and the alien conversed together in this way, and the astronaut was able to outline the purpose for his visit and receive encouraging responses in return. Alfie, meanwhile, proved to be a great hit with the children of the planet. They loved feeling his fur, listening to him bark and chasing him around the nearby streets. He was quite exhausted by the time Chuck and the alien had finished their conversation.

Chuck gave the aliens a great boxful of gifts from Earth that he had brought with him for that purpose.

"This is very primitive stuff," whistled an alien to Alfie. "Still, it might amuse the children for a few days."

The aliens gave a boxful of their items to Chuck to take back to Earth. These proved to be so sophisticated and advanced that when the spaceship returned there nobody back home knew what any of it was for.

Once the spaceship had set off on its return journey, Chuck turned to Alfie. "I did really well back there, didn't I? I was a great success and even you were useful, keeping the children amused."

Alfie sighed, content in the knowledge that once again he had saved the day.

Chapter 5

Alfie continued to travel with Chuck on his exploratory missions and also continued to save the day on numerous occasions. He found, for some strange reason, that he was better able to communicate with most aliens than Chuck. There was one planet where the aliens were strange, tall, thin stick-men and Alfie had a problem understanding them, but that had been the only occasion so far.

They had just returned from a really successful visit to Galixia, where Chuck had organised exchange visits for the alien teenagers with students from Earth, when Harry called him into his office.

Chuck reappeared some time later with a huge, beaming smile on his face. "Hey, guess what, Alfie? Bill's returning to work next week. I won't have to drag you all over the universe any more. I bet you'll be pleased to be staying at home in your nice, warm basket with Mrs Daykin to feed you doggy treats all day!"

Alfie's heart sank. He enjoyed being dragged all over the universe. And, more to the point, how would Chuck manage without him? In Alfie's opinion, it was nothing short of a miracle that Chuck had managed to escape serious injury for so long. The months of travelling with Chuck had convinced Alfie that his master was in need of a minder and that minder should be HIM! This needed some serious thinking.

Chuck was puzzled by Alfie's behaviour over the next few days. The dog wasn't interested in walkies and just lay in his basket with a dreamy expression on his face. In fact, Alfie was working hard to think up a plan of action that would enable him to continue to travel in the spaceship with Chuck. It seemed to him that the only solution was to become a stowaway, but how was he going to get on to the spaceship? After several days of serious thought, Alfie had devised a plan. It was risky, but it was his only chance of staying with Chuck.

The night before his next mission, Chuck started to pack his large trunk with everything he would need on the trip. While he was fetching his toiletries from the bathroom, Alfie grabbed his own space helmet by the strap and carried it over to the trunk. He buried the helmet underneath all of Chuck's clothes, then hid a number of sachets of dog food alongside it.

The following day Chuck loaded the car with his trunk, then came to say goodbye to Alfie. "Mrs Daykin will be here for you soon, Alfie," Chuck told the dog. "You can get out through the dog-flap if you need the garden. I'll see you in a few weeks." He patted Alfie lovingly, then went out of the kitchen and shut the door.

As quick as a flash Alfie leapt out of his basket, through the dog-flap and round to the front of the house. He dived through the open car door and hid behind the driver's seat. He heard Chuck climb in, whistling, shut the door, start the engine and pull out of the driveway. So far, so good!

At the space station, Chuck always left the car for the compound workers to unpack. They were so used to seeing Alfie that they did not think his presence was in any way strange. "Morning, space cadet," one of them said, patting Alfie on the head.

Keeping low on the ground, Alfie made his way to the store room. A huge trailer on wheels was waiting to be taken to the spaceship. It was full of the supplies the astronauts would need for their journey.

Making sure that no one was looking, Alfie clambered into the trailer and hid himself under the supplies. Some time later, a couple of compound workers came to tow the trailer to the spaceship. While they were taking the first load on board, Alfie climbed out and hid in the shadow of the craft. Once the men had completed their task and were towing the trailer back to the compound, Alfie emerged from his hiding-place. He galloped up the steps and made his way to the sleeping section, where he burrowed under some bedclothes, out of view.

Some time later Alfie heard Chuck and Bill come on board the spaceship. "Welcome back," said Chuck. "I sure have missed you, although Alfie made a good substitute. He was quite the blossoming astronaut."

When they were safely in orbit, Chuck and Bill unbuckled and began to sort out their trunks and stow away their clothes. "What the devil?" Alfie heard Chuck say.

"What's up, buddy?" asked Bill.

"Alfie's space helmet and some sachets of dog food are in my trunk. What on earth are they doing in there and who put them in?"

Alfie decided that this was an appropriate time to reveal his presence. Struggling out of the bedclothes, he launched himself at Chuck, barking and wagging his tail.

"What the …" Chuck nearly fell over in surprise. "Well, I never!" he exclaimed.

"Can you believe this, Bill? The dog obviously wants to be an astronaut after all."

And so it was that Alfie accompanied the two men on their space journey and continued to travel with them on all their future missions. The boss, Harry, decided that any dog who was that determined to stay with his master deserved a place in the spaceship.

Follow-up work for each chapter

CHAPTER 1

Put the children into mixed-ability groups of 5–6. Ask them to discuss and make notes on how they think aliens would describe humans. Let each group in turn read their notes to the others. What were the similarities and differences in their notes?

CHAPTER 2

Ask the children to draw and describe an alien life-form from an imaginary planet.

CHAPTER 3

In pairs, ask the children to design a meal for aliens that they think would best illustrate what humans like to eat. This could either be a buffet or a set meal with several courses. They can either write out a menu or draw plates with the relevant food on and label them.

CHAPTER 4

Chuck tried to do sign language to the aliens. With a partner, ask the children to work out some hand signs for everyday objects or activities. They can then take turns to show signs for the others to guess what they are depicting.

CHAPTER 5

Put the children into mixed-ability groups of 6. Ask them to work out and practise a short scene in which astronauts land on a strange planet. What happens when they encounter the native life-forms? How do they communicate? Do they get on? Is there a happy outcome?

Ideas for maths work

Shapes design

Ask the children to use mathematical shapes, drawn accurately with a ruler or round 2-D shapes – such as squares, rectangles, circles, triangles – to design a spacecraft and space station.

Space symmetry

Photocopy the symmetrical shapes template, 2.1 (p. 48) on to A3 paper, one copy for each child. Ask children to complete the shapes. Keep the completed rockets to play the two-dice activity.

Alien puzzle

Tell the children that the aliens have set them a puzzle to complete. Get them to work in mixed-ability pairs. Using squared paper, they need to cut out five 1cm squares. Ask them to see how many different shapes they can make with the five squares (there are 12 shapes – see below). Ask them to cut out each shape. You can show all the shapes once the children have had an opportunity to work them out for themselves. Explain to the children that the alien puzzle is to create a rectangle 6 squares wide by 10 squares deep using their shapes as a jigsaw.

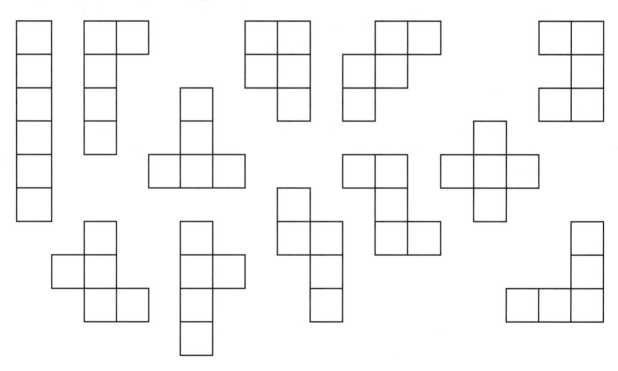

Science activities

Make a spacecraft

Put the children into pairs and ask them to design and make a spacecraft, paying particular attention to its aerodynamic properties. Hold a competition to see which spacecraft flies the furthest.

Strongest paper

Explain to the children that some aliens who are visiting Earth are fascinated by all the different types of paper we have. They want to find out which paper is strongest. Ask the children to set up an experiment to test various types of paper (e.g. tissue, computer, sugar, crepe, tracing). They need to cut paper strips 30cm by 1cm (make sure they are no wider than this, otherwise some of the strips may be too strong for the experiment). One end of each strip should be stuck with sticky tape to the edge of a table so that the paper hangs free. The children need to find a way of attaching the other end of each strip firmly to a container (e.g. a yoghurt pot). The children put weights or marbles into each container in turn and see how many are needed before the paper tears. They record their result for each strip to see which paper can hold the greatest weight.

Other activities

Two-dice rockets

Show the children how to cut up their rockets from the 'Space symmetry' activity into 12 parts. They should number the parts 2 to 12, repeating one of the numbers (so that all 12 parts have a number written on them). This activity is done with a partner or in a small group. They take turns to throw two dice and add the scores to give a total – they must not use the two numbers separately. (If the children can't manage to add the scores of two dice, they can divide their rockets into six parts and just use one dice.)

They take the rocket part that displays the same number as their dice total to form part of their rocket. The object of the game is to be the first to complete their rocket. If they achieve a dice total for which they already have the rocket part, they do not have another go but wait for their next turn.

Space shapes

Photocopy the space shapes template, 2.2 (p. 49), on to A3 paper so the shapes can be displayed for the whole class to see. Tell the children to try to use each shape in a space picture. They can rotate a shape or incorporate it as part of another shape.

Space crossword

Photocopy the crossword template, 2.3 (p. 50), for each child.

Space quiz

Give out the quiz sheet, template 2.4 (p. 51), either individually or in pairs.

Find the space words

The children use the 'Find the space words' template, 2.5 (p. 52).

Space missions

Give each child a copy of template 2.6 (p. 53). The instructions are on the sheet.

Active games

Alien relay

Divide the class into two evenly matched teams. The teams stand in a large circle. One child from each team begins the action by weaving in and out of their team-mates around the circle in a clockwise direction. When the child returns to their space, the player on their left sets off, and so on until each team member has had a turn. When the last player returns to their space in the circle their team sits down. The first team whose members all complete the circuit is the winner.

Spaceships

Put the children into groups of 3, with one child left over. Two children in each group form a spaceship by facing each other and holding hands. The third child is the astronaut and stands inside the spaceship. The game is played by astronauts contacting one another, using signs or winks and so on, to swap spaceships. The lone child without a spaceship must watch for a swap-over and try to steal a spaceship. Any spare children can be astronauts looking for a spaceship if the numbers don't work exactly. If successful, a new child becomes the lone astronaut. Warn the children that those forming the spaceships cannot refuse entry to an astronaut. Change the children round during the activity, so that each child has a turn at being an astronaut.

Aliens versus humans

The children stand in a large circle. Label them 'alien' and 'human' alternately round the circle. Give one large ball to an alien and another to a human on the opposite side of the circle. On your command, each team member passes the ball to the next member of their team (i.e. human to human, alien to alien) around the circle in a clockwise direction. In other words, they must pass the ball in front of the children from the opposing team. The first team to pass the ball around the circle and back to the beginning is the winner. If the children find this easy, get them to try passing the ball behind their backs.

Alien chief

The children sit in a large circle. Choose one child to leave the room briefly while you choose an alien chief. The alien chief is to perform actions that the other children must copy (e.g. tapping their knees, clapping, standing on one leg). Once an action is established, the child outside is invited back into the room to stand in the centre of the circle. The object of the game is for the child in the centre to guess who the alien chief is. The alien chief must try to change the action without being spotted. Tell the children to try not to look directly at the alien chief as that will give the game away. Allow the child in the centre two guesses, then play the game again with different participants.

Aliens walking

Put the children into groups of 4–5, evenly matched in height if possible. Tell them they are alien monsters. Get each group to form a line, one behind the other, each child except the first grasping the waist of the child in front. They are going to try to march in unison, so all the children put their right foot forward together, then their left foot forward together. Give them some time to practise, then ask each group to demonstrate their monster's walk. Next ask each group to form a circle with their backs facing inwards. They link arms around their circles and try to move across the room in unison. They must be careful not to pull any child over.

Art

Spacecraft designs

Ask each child to design the exterior and interior of a spacecraft, putting in all the features they consider important for space travel.

Solar system

This activity can be completed in groups or as a whole-class project. Ask the children to create a mobile of a solar system. If this is 2-D, they can cut circles of various sizes to represent a sun and planets. Encourage them to make their artwork interesting by creating textured surfaces (e.g. with scrunched-up tissue paper, scraps of material, wool, string, glitter or the netting from bags of fruit) and using chalks and pastels to create blended colours.

If you want to use this activity throughout the week, the children can make 3-D planets by sticking papier mâché over a partially inflated balloon.

Moon-base

Create a lunar surface on a large board by covering scrunched-up newspaper with Polyfilla®. When the surface is dry, it can be painted grey. Encourage the children to create a moon-base with buildings made from cardboard boxes, and with rockets and spacecraft. If they want, they can add aliens made from air-drying clay, then painted.

Shadow puppets

Put the children into small groups. Ask each child in the group to make a card puppet of an astronaut or an alien with jointed arms that are attached at the shoulder and elbow with split pins. Each puppet needs three sticks attached, one to the body and one to each hand. The children hold and move the sticks to create action in their puppets. Ask the children to make up and practise a short play involving their puppets. Let each group perform their shadow play by shining a bright light on to the puppets in front of a blank wall or sheet.

Space symmetry

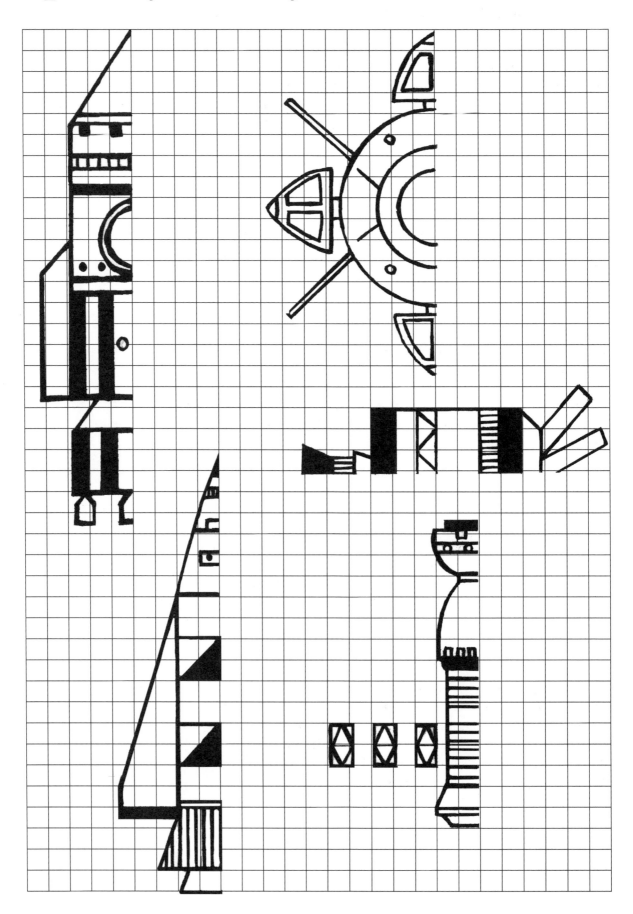

Space shapes

Space crossword

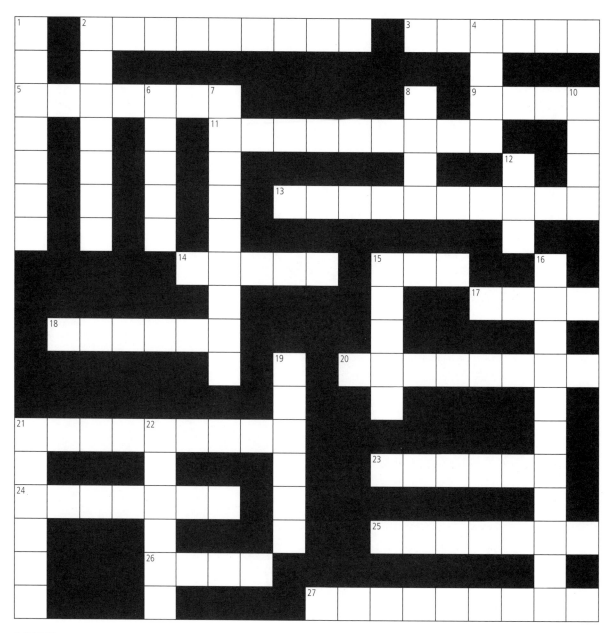

ACROSS

2 You need to wear one when you leave our planet (9)
3 This planet has rings (6)
5 These large bodies orbit the sun (7)
9 You see it in the sky at night (4)
11 The name for a person who travels in space (9)
13 The layer of gas around our planet (10)
14 The name given to a being from another planet (5)
15 Lift ___ is the start of a journey in space (3)
17 Does a man live in this feature of the night sky? (4)
18 A jet-propelled engine that powers a spacecraft (6)
20 Not a drink or a sweet, but a spiral of stars (5, 3)
21 Astronauts may train in this machine (9)
23 A collection of millions of stars (6)
24 The planet that is nearest to the sun (7)
25 The force or pull exerted by Earth (5)
26 The top end of a rocket is its nose ____ (4)
27 The study of things beyond our planet (9)

DOWN

1 The largest planet in our solar system (7)
2 A rocket waiting to begin its journey is on this (5,2)
4 Carried out before a space flight (4)
6 The planet we live on (5)
7 A man-made object that is in orbit (9)
8 Do little green men live here? (4)
10 The space ____ is the rush to explore the universe (4)
12 The astrological sign of the lion (3)
15 A planet's path round the sun is its _____ (5)
16 The name for the sun and its planets (5, 6)
19 Force that makes a rocket lift off (6)
21 The season when we see the sun most (6)
22 Makes a rocket take off (6)

2.4

Space quiz

Find the answers to the clues below and take the first letter from each answer.
Unscramble the letters to make a space word.

1. Something children love to eat between meals   __ __ __ __ __ __

A ball game in which players pick up the ball and run with it   __ __ __ __ __

A crunchy red or green fruit   __ __ __ __ __

A little furry animal that squeaks and likes cheese   __ __ __ __ __

Write the first letters here   __ __ __ __
Unscramble them to find the answer to this clue. Little green men are supposed to live
on this planet   __ __ __ __.

2. A round juicy fruit that has the same colour as its name   __ __ __ __ __ __

A bird that flies at night and hoots   __ __ __

The opposite of day   __ __ __ __ __

An animal that swings from the branches of trees   __ __ __ __ __ __

Write the first letters here   __ __ __ __
Unscramble the letters to find the answer to this clue.
You can see this at night   __ __ __ __.

3. This puzzle is in two parts that make one word.

Part 1   An animal with a curly tail that grunts   __ __ __

These are fluffy and white in the sky   __ __ __ __ __ __

A tiny insect that lives in colonies in the garden   __ __ __

Some people like this boiled or fried for breakfast   __ __ __

Cinderella had a glass one   __ __ __ __ __ __ __

Part 2   The opposite of cold   __ __ __

What frozen water is called   __ __ __

The opposite of hard   __ __ __ __

You find this little brown thing in the middle of an apple.
Its name reads the same both ways.   __ __ __.

Write the first letters here   __ __ __ __ __ / __ __ __ __.
Unscramble the letters in each part separately to find the answer to this clue.
You might need this for space explorations   __ __ __ __ __ __ __ __.

Make up some clues for words with a partner. Below are some ideas for space words:
Comet, planet, Jupiter, star, Milky Way, asteroid.

2.5

Find the space words

Each number corresponds to a letter in the wheel below.
Solve the sums to find each letter, then unscramble the letters to make space words.

1 (6+8) (13−7) (15+5) (6+5)   V __ __ __ __

2 (18+7) (22−11) (19−14) (5+9)   A __ __ __ __

3 (7+4) (36−25) (20−12) (5×2) (9+9)   M __ __ __ __ __

4 (30÷3) (4×2) (17−6) (5+7) (25−10)   R __ __ __ __ __

5 (3+7) (9×2) (15+10) (2+9) (30−23) (12÷6)   J __ __ __ __ __ __

6 (16÷2) (43−33) (4×4) (30−5) (2×4) (5+9) (20−11) /

(12−9) (60÷6) (11+7)   S __ __ __ __ __ __ __ /S __ __ __

7 (5×3) (5×5) (20÷4) (8+5) / (12÷4) (19−6)   M __ __ __ __ /W __ __

8 (14÷2) (28−16) (22÷2) (30÷10) / (8×2) (22−15) (31−6)   S __ __ __ __ /S __ __ __

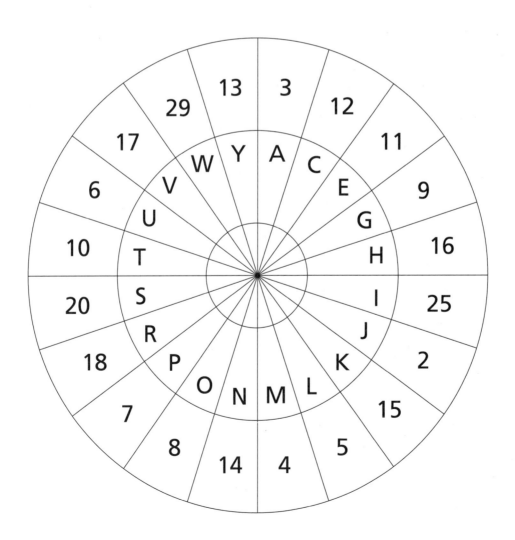

Space missions

Add up the weeks in the planets to see which space craft reached its destination first.
If you would like to, have a go at the days in the stars to see how long they took to
get back again.

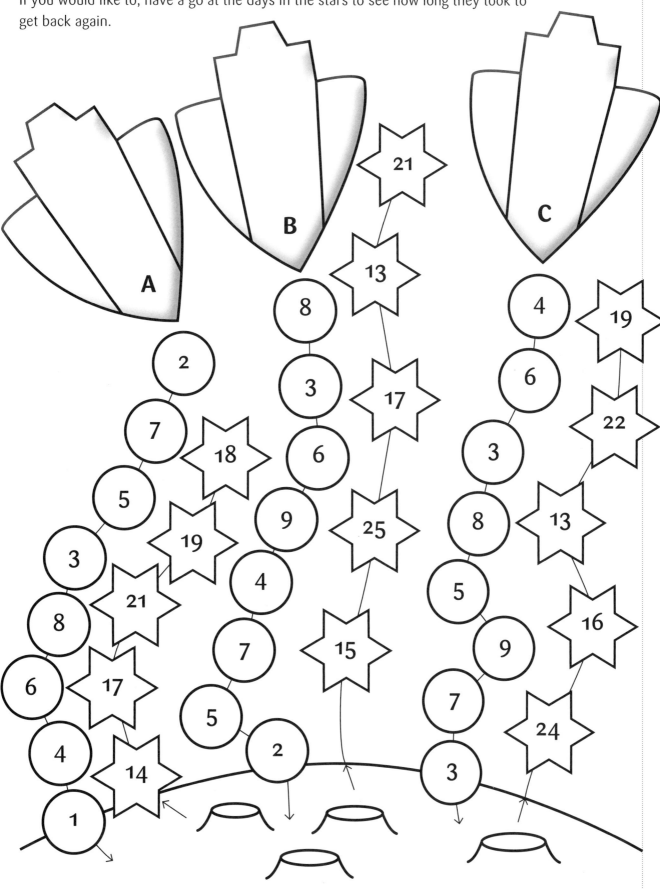

Elsie, the Wizard

A story of magic and evil-doing
in the hamlet of Rudge

Chapter 1

The hamlet of Rudge, in Somerset, is so small that people could drive through without noticing it at all. There are only 50 inhabitants and the houses are well spread out, so they do not give the impression of being a community. You would probably think it was a dull sort of place, full of contented, munching cows and placid country folk, where very little ever happened to upset the natural rhythm of the seasons. But in this you would be quite wrong, for the hamlet has its share of crises and good and bad people, as much as any large city.

Twins Kelsey and Kieron lived in Middle Rudge, in an old cottage with an inglenook fire-place. Their house was surrounded by fields that they could play in and where they could discover all sorts of interesting, natural artefacts and make up great adventures. Their mother, Mrs Burnett, had befriended an old man, Leslie Heward, who was a widower and lived alone in the village. He seemed to be away a lot of the time, but when he was at home Mrs Burnett helped him with his housework and shopped for him. Sometimes Kelsey and Kieron visited to enjoy a few hours of squash, cakes and interesting chatter with the old man.

Leslie Heward seemed to know an awful lot about everything. He was always entertaining and fun to be with and never talked down to the twins – in fact, they had never met anyone of his age before who was such good company. Also, he had two very friendly and cuddly cats called Pyewacket and Sheba that the children liked to stroke and play with.

One afternoon they went to visit Leslie to discuss something they had witnessed concerning a neighbour of theirs. This was a relative newcomer to the hamlet, called Mrs Kite, who lived alone save for a dozen mangy-looking cats. They certainly weren't sleek and well fed like Leslie's pair of moggies and they were decidedly unfriendly – as was their owner. Mrs Kite never spoke to the twins if they happened to pass in the hamlet and barely managed a civil 'Morning' to their parents.

"Well, the thing is, Leslie," said Kieron one day, "we were playing in Four-acre Field earlier and we heard Mrs Kite talking in a cross voice. We wondered who on earth she could have been telling off, so we crept up to peep through the hedge. You just wouldn't believe what we saw. Mrs Kite was shouting at her CATS and they were all sat down looking at her, as if they were listening properly to what she was saying."

"And," Kelsey butted in, "you wouldn't believe what she was saying either."

The young girl thought again of the dreadful words that she had heard Mrs Kite speaking. "I'm not at all satisfied with you," she had shouted at the silent animals in front of her. "The information you've been bringing me is worthless. I want some decent spying done and not of people's gardens. What I need is inside information, conversations reported, the letters people receive, the sort of thing I can blackmail people with. If I am going to be all-powerful here, I need to know everyone's personal business, not the useless tittle-tattle you've been bringing me. In future you are going to have to earn your keep. No decent information – no food!"

One of the cats, a battle-scarred ginger tom, had tentatively raised a paw and mewed several times to Mrs Kite.

"So, you get chased away all the time, do you, by the people and their cats? Hmm," she had replied and had stood in thought for several minutes. Then an evil smile had lit up her face as she cried, "Well then, we'll have to solve that problem by getting rid of all their cats so that I can kindly offer them a replacement. Mr Brownlow is crop spraying this week. I'll poison all the cats and blame it on the chemicals in the spray. Of course, I shall have to say that I've always considered it a dangerous practice and so I kept my cats safely indoors. With you lot as pets inside the homes, I'll be able to find out everything I need to know."

Kelsey relayed all this to the old man, then added, "Your cats are in terrible danger and so is our little Mimi, but how can Mrs Kite talk to and understand her cats?"

"Ah well," Leslie answered her, "it's not so difficult if you know how, and this has confirmed my suspicions about that woman. You see, my dears, Mrs Kite is obviously a witch, and an evil one at that."

The twins gasped in dismay and looked very frightened and a bit tearful.

"Don't worry," Leslie reassured them, "I haven't reached my grand age without picking up lots of useful information on the way. It's really not as bad as you think."

"There's more," added Kieron. "Mrs Kite sent the cats away to collect things for her, like ragwort plants, blackbirds' eggs, adders' tongues and newts' tails."

"Ha, I know exactly what she is going to make and I know the perfect antidote," said Leslie. "However, I don't have any here, so I am going to need your help in this matter. Unfortunately, it means that one of you must go alone somewhere to collect the antidote, while the other remains here to help me. It's quite safe where I'm sending you and my cat Sheba will show you the way."

The twins looked at each other, unsure of what to say or do. Sheba brushed against Kelsey's legs and mewed at her. "I'll go," Kelsey said. She felt that was what the cat wanted.

"Well done," said Leslie. "Now if you follow me I'll set you on your way."

Chapter 2

Leslie led the two children across the garden to his garage, which he always kept locked. Taking the key out of his pocket, he opened the door and led the children inside, shutting the door behind them immediately. Kelsey wondered if he was going to drive her somewhere after all, but the old man motioned for the children to follow him towards the rear of the garage. The front half, which housed the car, was like a normal garage, but the far end was like nothing the children had ever seen before.

This area was set out like a laboratory with shelves of books, scientific instruments and bottles of many-coloured liquids. On one wall hung a large chart covered in strange symbols and complex diagrams, below which was a table overflowing with papers and smaller charts. In one corner was a narrow door that caught the twins' attention.

"That's funny," said Kieron, "I've never noticed that door from the outside."

Giving them a strange look, Leslie pushed open the door and the children could see the view beyond. It wasn't the field outside the garage, that much was certain. "Come, Kelsey," beckoned Leslie. "This is your means of entry into the outer land." He laughed at her puzzled expression. "Oh, there are lots of things about me that you don't know. Now, don't be afraid. Sheba will take great care of you. I wouldn't let you go if I thought you'd come to any harm. Sheba is going to guide you to the house of Elsiel the wizard. That's where the antidote is. I will give you a note to take there. You'll find his apprentice Faisal very pleasant and helpful too."

Leslie gently propelled Kelsey through the open door, "Now off you go," he encouraged. "There's not a moment to lose."

Kelsey found herself in the strangest place she had ever seen. She was standing in a large forest full of the most unusual trees. They were clad in barks of various shades of red and pink, from deep crimson and bright scarlet, through salmon pink to cerise. Their leaves were vivid and multi-coloured, so the whole area had the appearance of an exotic jungle. Sheba mewed at Kelsey, then set off down a path that ran through the forest.

They had been walking for about 30 minutes when they reached a clearing in the trees. A charming cottage nestled among flowering shrubs. Sheba walked up to the cottage and sat in front of the door. Nervously, Kelsey lifted the door knocker and rapped three times. She wondered if the wizard Elsiel would be large and scary.

The door opened and a face peered out. It belonged to a young boy, a few years older than Kelsey.

"Excuse me, are you Elsiel the wizard?" asked Kelsey.

The young boy laughed. "Do I look like a wizard?" he asked. "No, I'm his apprentice, Faisal. Elsiel's away at the moment and won't be back till next week."

Kelsey felt a sinking feeling in the pit of her stomach. What was she to do? The antidote was needed urgently or everyone would lose their much loved pet. She handed Faisal the note, saying, "Can you help me, then? It's really urgent that I take this antidote back with me. A wicked witch is going to poison all the cats in our village."

Faisal read the note, then said, "Oh yes. This is very easy and straightforward. Come in and sit down while I prepare it for you."

Kelsey perched on a stool while Faisal bustled about the room collecting a variety of ingredients from jars and bottles, which he placed in a large pan with a lock-down lid. He fiddled with various dials and knobs and the pan began to make a whirring sound.

"We'll just leave that to brew for ten minutes," he said. "Would you like a drink?" They sat together with the most delicious and refreshing drink that Kelsey had ever tasted. It seemed to contain every single flavour that she liked the most.

Faisal wore a gold brooch on his tunic with a large blue stone in its centre. "That's so beautiful," Kelsey commented.

"It's very useful too," Faisal told her. "When there is any danger about, the stone turns red to warn you." Wanting to impress the young girl with his magical prowess, he continued, "I've all sorts of useful things. Look at this."

He produced a ring from a pouch dangling from his waist and slipped it on to a finger. Immediately, he disappeared.

Kelsey gasped. "Faisal, where are you?" she shouted.

"Right next to you," came the reply. "That ring made me invisible." A grinning Faisal reappeared.

A ping from the pan interrupted their conversation. "Antidote's ready," Faisal said, lifting the lid. He reached into the pan and pulled out a handful of brown tablets.

"Here you are," he said, holding out his hand for Kelsey to examine the contents.

"My cat hates taking tablets," Kelsey told Faisal. "What if we can't get the cats to swallow these?"

"Take a sniff," commanded the boy. Kelsey leaned forwards and smelled the tablets.

"Phew!" she exclaimed. "They've got a sort of fishy, mousy smell."

"Exactly," Faisal replied. "They have all of a cat's favourite scents to make them desirable. Believe me, no cat will refuse one of these."

Faisal put the tablets into a jar with a screw-top lid, then turned to Kelsey. "As you're in a hurry, I'll show you a short-cut back," he told her. "You'll be home in no time at all."

"I wonder how Kieron and Leslie are getting on back in Rudge," Kelsey thought aloud. "I hope everything is going well for them."

Chapter 3

Back in Rudge, Leslie had thought of a cunning plan to hold up the cats in their ingredients collecting.

"Hop in the car," he told Kieron. The next minute they were driving up the hill and out of the hamlet. Leslie parked the car on the road and, with Kieron in tow, started to walk down the narrow lane that led to Rudge Manor.

"What I am about to do would, in normal circumstances, be very wrong. However, desperate deeds call for desperate measures," said the old man. He dived through a gap in the hedge and skirted round the manor house to a set of buildings at the rear of the property. A terrible racket came from the buildings. Kieron knew what it was: dogs barking. The buildings housed the hounds that the local huntsman used to follow trails.

"I want you to stay here and keep watch," Leslie said to Kieron. "If you see anybody, give a loud whistle. OK?" Kieron nodded his assent, and Leslie left him and walked towards the kennels. He opened the gate to their compound and let the dogs out. It seemed to Kieron, watching, that Leslie was deep in conversation with the hounds, but that had to be absurd, didn't it? Anyway, within a few minutes the hounds dispersed in every direction and Leslie returned.

"Well," he chuckled, "they're off to keep Mrs Kite's cats occupied for a while. That should hold up her potion-making until we have the antidote. Now, young man," he continued, "we're going to do some collecting of our own. I have in mind something very special to make that will deal with Mrs Kite once and for all."

Meanwhile, in the outer land, Faisal and Kelsey were making their way back through the red forest. Unfortunately, the pair were so deep in conversation that the young apprentice had missed one of the small tracks on the short-cut and they had strayed away from their intended route. They were suddenly confronted by a steep hill, at the bottom of which stood the smallest and most exquisite castle Kelsey had ever seen. It was almost like a large Wendy house with tiny turrets and battlements in perfect proportion.

"Who lives in that beautiful little castle?" Kelsey enquired.

"I don't know," replied Faisal. "I've never seen it before."

He looked puzzled and scratched his head. "I think we've strayed off the track. We'll have to retrace our steps to get back on the right path."

Kelsey looked at the castle again. She imagined its owner to be a lovely princess and her curiosity was aroused. "I just want to take a really quick peep at the castle, "she said, and before Faisal could protest she ran down the hill, shouting, "I'll be ever so quick, I promise."

As she approached the moat that surrounded the castle, which twinkled silver in the sunlight, the door of the castle opened and out stepped a woman no bigger than Kelsey herself. Waves of soft, snow-white hair framed a face as round and rosy as an apple. Dressed in a longish, pale-blue dress covered in a white lace-edged apron, she was the picture of every child's ideal grandma. She held a wicker basket over one arm and began to walk around her well-stocked garden, selecting the most perfect blooms to cut and place in the basket. As she looked up at the approaching child, a smile like a summer's day lit up her face.

"Good morning, my dear," she said to Kelsey. "I see that you are admiring my little castle. Perhaps you'd like to come inside and see the rest of it. I have many beautiful objects. Then we could enjoy a glass of cherry squash and cake together."

"Thank you, that's very kind of you," Kelsey answered, "but I'm in a terrible hurry today. Perhaps I could come for a visit another time."

The old lady smiled sweetly and said, "Well, at least let me give you one of my magic flowers. It will bring you good luck."

It was just at this precise moment that Faisal noticed something alarming. The stone of his brooch had changed from its normal blue colour and was pulsing bright, red waves of light. He began to run towards the young girl, shouting, "No, Kelsey, stop! Stop! Don't go into the garden. It's dangerous." But his words were carried away on the wind. He watched in dismay as Kelsey reached out a hand to take the proffered flower.

With an unexpected swiftness that took Kelsey by surprise, the old lady sprang forwards and clasped her wrist in a vice-like grip. Before the child had time to realise what was happening, the old lady had dragged her into the castle and slammed the door shut, locking it securely with a large iron key that she removed from her apron pocket.

"Elsiel put a spell on me because he thought I was causing too much mischief in the outer land. If I venture out of my garden I will be turned to stone, so for years I've been alone with no help or companionship. But I knew that if I made my castle and garden attractive, one day some foolish person would walk in. And here you are! Now I will have a servant and some company." The old lady cackled in a horrible, cracked voice.

The inside of the castle was nothing like the exterior. It was dark, drab and dirty. Kelsey looked around her in horror, and the full realisation of the evil crone's words hit her.

Not only had she failed in her quest to bring back the antidote for Leslie and save the cats of Rudge, but she would never see her family again.

The old lady set her to work immediately, scrubbing and polishing. When it was time for bed and Kelsey was exhausted, her captor chained her to the leg of a table and threw her a smelly old blanket for a cover.

"Oh yes," she told the weeping child, "you'll make the perfect servant."

Chapter 4

After two hours of collecting, Leslie was satisfied that they had all the ingredients he required. At intervals during this time, they had heard the excited yelps and barks of the hounds as they harried Mrs Kite's cats up hill and down dale. "I don't think Mrs Kite will have the ingredients she needs for a few hours yet," he chuckled.

Back in his garage, Leslie emptied the ingredients on to a table and he and Kieron spent the next half-hour cutting and chopping. Everything went into a large pot, just like the one in Elsiel's cottage, and then the old man added several more things from the pots and jars on the shelves.

"This is a very powerful potion, so it's going to take some time to brew. I learnt about it from my friend Elsiel. It won't be ready until tomorrow, but that will be fine. Kelsey should be back very soon now with the antidote, so the cats of Rudge will be safe for the time being."

Unfortunately, that was not the case. Kelsey was chained, tired and weeping, to a table leg with little hope of escape. The old crone busied herself with her night-time ritual, making a hot drink and filling a hot-water bottle for her bed. She was just about to retire for the night when there was a strange scratching sound at the door of the castle.

"What on earth is that?" She stopped to listen. The scratching came again. Muttering under her breath, the old lady removed a large sharp knife from her kitchen drawer, and armed with this weapon she unlocked the door and pulled it open just enough to peer out. Seeing nothing, she opened the door wide and stepped outside.

"Most peculiar," she muttered as she re-entered the castle. "Nothing there!" She relocked the door, then turned to Kelsey. "I'm off to bed now," she told her. "You'd better get some sleep, you've got a busy day tomorrow." Cackling to herself, she disappeared into her bedroom. Within minutes, the sound of loud snoring could be heard.

Kelsey, alone in the kitchen, tried to make herself as comfortable as possible on the hard stone floor. It wasn't easy as she was cold and hungry. She thought she heard a slight rustling close by and sat up in alarm in case it was a rat.

The sight that met her eyes was most extraordinary. First a pair of feet appeared next to her, followed by a pair of legs, then a body and finally a head. Faisal's grinning face loomed close as he held up the invisibility ring for the girl to see. He placed his finger on his lips to indicate that she should be quiet, then leaning in he whispered to Kelsey, "Where does the old hag keep the keys to the door and your leg chain?"

"They're in her apron pocket," Kelsey whispered in reply.

Telling her to stay still, Faisal disappeared into the old lady's bedroom. The sound of snoring continued unabated. Within a minute he reappeared with the keys and unlocked the leg chain. Then the two tiptoed over to the door. The key made a grating sound in the lock and the pair held their breath in alarm, but the old lady's sleep was not disturbed. Faisal opened the door very slowly until there was sufficient space for them to squeeze through.

"Now, run!" he shouted to Kelsey as he slammed the door shut. The pair raced across the garden. As they reached the gate they heard angry shrieks from the old lady as she pursued them. However she was not fast enough, and Kelsey and Faisal made good their escape from the crone's property. Reaching the gate herself, she could only glare at them and scream her curses. Once they were well clear of the castle, Faisal slowed down to allow Kelsey to catch her breath.

"Oh, thank you for saving me," she said to him. "I don't know what I would have done without your help. Imagine being trapped there for ever with that nasty, old woman!"

"We must hurry," Faisal urged her, "we've wasted too much time already."

When Kelsey arrived back at the garage, she handed the tablets to Leslie, apologising for taking so long. "Elsiel wasn't at home, so his apprentice Faisal helped me," she told him, and proceeded to tell Leslie and Kieron about her frightening ordeal.

"Elsiel made a good choice in that young man. I'm told that he is hard working and learns quickly – luckily for you, Kelsey. I must have a word with Elsiel about that old woman, though. He will have to make sure that her castle and garden look as uninviting on the outside as they are on the inside, so that no one ever gets trapped by her again. Now, we have work to do."

Leslie instructed the pair in their task. They had to make sure that every cat in Rudge, excluding Mrs Kite's, had one of the tablets. This proved to be easier than they had thought as the delicious smell of the tablets was irresistible to the cats. Having completed their task, the twins returned home to keep an eye on proceedings in the neighbourhood. They saw a very irate Mr Brownlow of Rudge Manor taking his hounds back to their kennels. Kieron told Kelsey how Leslie had freed the dogs to hold up Mrs Kite's cats. Throughout the late afternoon, they saw the witch's cats returning one by one with things in their mouths.

"I suppose Mrs Kite will do her poisoning during the night," commented Kelsey, "but, thanks to Leslie and his friends, nobody's cat will be harmed."

"I can't wait to see her face when she realises that her evil plan hasn't worked," said Kieron. "I wonder what Leslie is planning for her."

"Well, we'll know tomorrow," Kelsey told him.

Chapter 5

The following day, bright and early, the twins presented themselves at Leslie's house. He led them into his kitchen, where they were soon seated around his table.

"We have some more cat tablets to dispense today," he told them, "but this time they are only for Mrs Kite's cats." He showed the children a container of green tablets. They smelt just as delicious – in cat terms, that is – as the brown ones had, but slightly differently.

"How will we give the cats these without Mrs Kite seeing us?" asked Kieron.

"I will call on Mrs Kite," said Leslie, "to discuss her contribution to the forthcoming Rudge fete. Don't worry, I can be a doddery old man and take absolutely ages getting everything right. As you saw with the brown tablets, there will be no trouble getting the cats to eat them. When you have given a tablet to every one of her cats, walk past the front of her house and call 'Hello' to me."

The plan was put into action. While Leslie engaged Mrs Kite in conversation by her front door, the children slipped through a gap in the hedge at the bottom of her garden. All the witch's cats were sprawled out on the grass, recovering from being chased around the hamlet the previous day by the hounds. At first, when they saw the children, their hackles rose and they glared at them menacingly and flexed their claws. However as soon as the scent of the tablets reached their nostrils, they calmed down and eagerly awaited their turn for the enticing treat. Within ten minutes, all the cats had been given a tablet. The children called a cheery, "Hello, Leslie," as they passed in front of Mrs Kite's cottage.

A short time later, they met back in Leslie's kitchen. "Time for squash and biscuits, I think," he said, "as we wait for the tablets to work."

An hour later, when Leslie judged the time was right, he led the twins into the garden. He held a strange object in one hand. "This is a special cat whistle. You won't be able to hear it, but the cats will, and because of the tablets you gave to Mrs Kite's cats, they will come to me."

He placed the whistle to his lips and blew, long and hard. He repeated this action several times and after five minutes, just as he had predicted, Mrs Kite's cats began to appear in his garden. Leslie turned to the children, "I have work to do here. I want you to go home and keep an eye on Mrs Kite's cottage. In half an hour or so, the fun will begin."

The twins left the old man's cottage. As they made their way home, Kelsey turned to Kieron with a worried expression. "I hope he doesn't kill the witch's cats," she said.

"Leslie wouldn't harm them. He loves animals," Kieron reassured her. He remembered how Leslie had seemed to converse with Mr Brownlow's hounds. "I'm sure he has a good plan. Don't worry."

Once the twins were back at their cottage, they went upstairs into Kieron's bedroom. From his window they had a good view of Mrs Kite's property. They saw her bustling about with an angry look on her face. She had obviously seen that her poisoning plan had failed. Stomping out into her garden, she called several of her cats – but they were nowhere to be seen. She stomped back into her cottage, and for the next half-hour she reappeared in the garden at ten-minute intervals to call her cats. Her face became more and more furious as they failed to appear.

The children continued to watch, and the fourth time that the witch came into her garden, they saw the furry shapes of her cats squeezing through gaps in the hedge, to line up in front of her. The twins could not hear her exact words, but from the volume and tone of her voice they knew Mrs Kite was shouting angrily at the cats. And then something very strange happened. The cats began to approach Mrs Kite menacingly. Together they flexed their claws and hissed at the witch. A puzzled expression crossed her face and she took a step backwards. In one furry, snarling movement, the cats launched themselves, biting and scratching at the surprised woman. After a moment's hesitation, Mrs Kite took off down the road with a pack of angry cats at her heels. The twins watched in amazement as she disappeared round a bend in the road and out of the hamlet.

"Come on," shouted Kieron, and the pair raced down the stairs out of the house and along the road to Leslie's house.

"Well?" he asked them, grinning. "Did you catch all the fun? That's the last we'll see of Mrs Kite in this village. She will realise that someone with magical powers knows what she's up to in Rudge, so she'll be off to pastures new with her wicked ways."

"But what will happen to her cats?" asked Kelsey.

"Don't worry about them," said Leslie. "Once they have chased her far enough away, they will come back to me. I intend to re-educate them into the ways of nice, family pets and then I will find loving homes for them. Come on," he added, "time for a celebration, I think. Squash and cream cakes all round!"

Later on that same day, Kieron and Kelsey were seated at the table eating dinner with their parents. Suddenly, Kieron exclaimed, "Do you know what, Kelsey? Leslie is an anagram of Elsiel and Leslie does go away quite often. I wonder …"

"What do you wonder?" asked their mother.

"Oh, nothing important," Kieron answered, but he and Kelsey exchanged knowing grins.

Follow-up work for each chapter

CHAPTER 1

Tell the children to imagine that a witch has moved into their road. She doesn't wear long black robes or a pointy hat as she wants to blend in and not be noticed. However there are tell-tale signs that let them know she is a witch. Ask the children to write or draw her, giving details about her appearance, life-style and habits that inform them she is a witch. What do they think her wicked plans are?

CHAPTER 2

Put the children in mixed-ability pairs. Ask them to imagine that one of them is a wizard and the other an apprentice, like Faisal. Tell them to work out a short scene in which the wizard is teaching the apprentice how to make a new magic potion. They must think of what the potion is for, what ingredients are needed and how to make it. They must make sure that both wizard and apprentice have things to say and do. Ask them to practise the magic lesson and act it out to the others in the class.

CHAPTER 3

Tell the children to imagine that they could have three objects with magical powers, like Faisal's brooch and ring. What would their objects be and what powers would they have?
Ask the children to draw and describe the three objects.

CHAPTER 4

Tell the children to imagine that they and a friend are trapped in a giant's castle.
Ask them to make a comic strip or write a story to show how they would manage to escape.

CHAPTER 5

Ask the children, in mixed-ability pairs, to devise a cunning plan to get rid of the witch in their road. They should make notes on everything they would need for this plan and on how they would carry it out.

Ideas for maths work

A magic trick

Explain to the children that you are going to show them a magic trick to amaze their friends. Put them into mixed-ability pairs or groups, so that help is available if needed. Prepare a piece of card 21cm by 15 cm, as shown in the diagram below. Show the children the blank side of the card and ask if they think you could step through the card. Turn the card over. Carefully cut along all the lines (or have a pre-cut card ready) and gently open out the rectangle. With care, you will be able to step through the opening. Ask the children to draw rectangles of the correct size accurately and make their own magic cards. You will need to draw a large version on the board for them to copy. If you think some children will have difficulty with this activity, you could photocopy the design on to card for them to cut out.

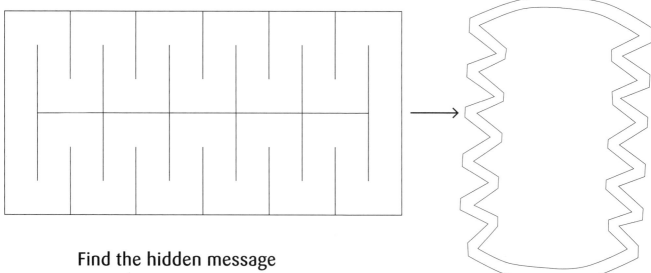

Find the hidden message

Photocopy the Find the hidden message template, 3.1 (p. 72), for each child.

Reach the enchanted castle

For this game you should put the children into pairs. Instructions for preparation are on template 3.2 (p. 73). Give each pair a copy.

Pathways through the forest

For this individual measuring activity photocopy the Pathways through the forest template, 3.3 (p. 74), for each child.

The wizard's journey

Photocopy the instruction sheet and grid on templates 3.4 and 3.5 (pp. 75 and 76) for each child.

Complete the magic squares

Give each child a copy of the magic squares template, 3.6 (p. 77). When they have completed the two grids, encourage them to devise their own magic square.

Science activities

Coloured leaves

Explain to the children that they are going to witness something 'magic'. You will need some leafy inner stalks of celery and three bottles of dark food colouring, such as red, blue and black. Make up three jars of coloured water with the food colourings and place a leafy stalk of celery in each. Place another stalk in plain water as a control. After a couple of hours the children will begin to see a tinge of different colour around the edges of the leaves. By the following day the change will be really pronounced. They can compare the stalks in the coloured water with the control. Talk to the children about what is happening and how plants 'drink'.

Magic indicator

Prior to the session, prepare an indicator by boiling red cabbage in water. Use the resulting coloured liquid. Ask the children, in small groups, to test a variety of substances in samples of the liquid (e.g. lemon, bicarbonate of soda). They are to write down what they discover.

Other activities

Magic potion

Photocopy the Magic potion colouring template, 3.7 (p. 78), for each child. Ask them to write on the cauldron the ingredients to create a potion to make people happy. They could include such things as a joke book, a hug, a smile, a teddy and a flower. They then colour in the picture and create and colour an appropriate border.

Spot the difference

Photocopy the Spot the difference template, 3.8 (p. 79), for each child. Tell them there are 14 differences between the pictures. They should mark each difference with a circle on the right-hand picture.

Race to the wizard's house

Photocopy the Race to the wizard's house template, 3.9 (p. 80), so that there is one copy for every two children. Put the children into pairs and let them colour the sheet together, then play the game. They will need a counter each and a dice. They can then swap partners and play with someone else.

Three in a row

A game for two players. Each player uses a different coloured pen. The children will need to create and number a 6 by 6 grid (see below). They need two dice to play. They take turns to throw the dice and arrange the two numbers they get as a coordinate. They put an X on the grid in the relevant spot. The object of the game is to create a row of 3 Xs vertically, horizontally or diagonally. If a player throws a number which makes a coordinate that has an X on it already, they miss a turn.

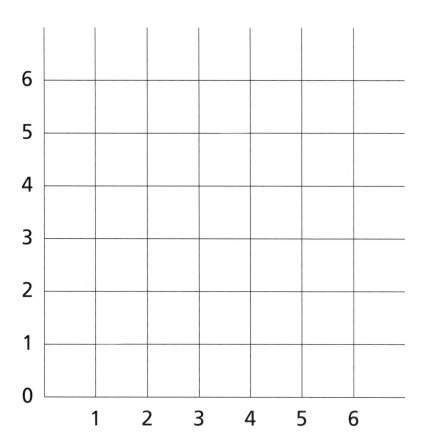

Active games

The wizard's apprentices

Put the children into two or three teams. Tell them that they are the wizard's apprentices. Each team should make up a name for their wizard. Tell the children that their wizards want them to get into height order, from the tallest to the shortest, on your command. The first team to achieve this is the winner. Next, they must arrange themselves in alphabetical order of first names.

Spells

Put the children into mixed-ability teams of 5 or 6. They stand in line, one behind the other, in their teams. The child standing at the front of each team has a whiteboard and pen. Tell the children they are going to play a game about ingredients for spells. Ask the children at the back of each line to come to you and show them a 3- to 6-letter word, without the other children seeing. The children must not say this word. They return to the back of their line. On your command they draw the first letter of the word on the back of the child in front with their forefinger. Each child, in turn, writes the same letter on the back of the child in front until it reaches the child with the whiteboard and pen. They write the letter on their board. The child at the back then writes the second letter on the back of the child in front, and this is passed down the line. This continues until the entire word has been written. Ask the children at the front to hold up their whiteboards to see if they have written the word down correctly. The child at the back of the line then goes up to the front and the game continues with a new word being shown. Continue until all the children have had a turn at writing on the whiteboard. Some ideas for words are: bat, frog, snake, weed, poison, spider.

Magic word race

Ask the children to bring in a selection of newspapers and magazines. Get them to cut out the headlines. Put the children into mixed-ability teams of 4–6, and put each team round a table with scissors, glue sticks, a large sheet of paper and a selection of headlines. Explain that you are going to put magic words on the board, one at a time. The teams must cut out the relevant letters from headlines and stick them on to their sheets of paper. It is up to each team how they organise task sharing. The first team to finish each word receives a point.

Some ideas for words: witch, wizard, spell book, wand, dragon, fairy.

Rescue teams

You will need props such as skipping-ropes, small PE mats, garden canes and plenty of space for this game. Put the children into mixed-ability groups of 6. One member of each group stands at the far end of the area, opposite the rest of their team. Explain to the children that there is a magic bog separating the lone child from their group. Each team must work together to devise a way of rescuing their team member, using the props available. No one may stand on the boggy ground.

Look at the dragon

The children sit or stand in a circle. One child is chosen to be the dragon, and lies down in the centre of the circle wearing a blindfold. A noisy object such as a set of bells or bunch of keys is placed by the dragon. Indicate to a child in the circle that they are to take the dragon's treasure and return to their seat. All the children place their hands behind their backs. The dragon removes the blindfold and has two guesses at who has taken the treasure. Repeat with a new dragon.

Art

Spatter pictures

Give the children an A5 piece of card and ask them to draw and cut out a 'magic' shape. Explain that this could be as complex as a witch on a broomstick or as simple as a cat, a witch's hat or a cauldron. The children fasten their shape on to an A4 sheet of black sugar paper with Blu-Tack®. Using a stiff paintbrush or old toothbrush, they flick bright-coloured paint on to the black paper, making sure they surround their shape with paint. When the paint has dried, the children remove their cardboard shape to reveal a black image left on the sugar paper.

Witch's cauldron

Make a table display with a cauldron (you could either use a Hallowe'en cauldron or cut a shape from thick card). Ask the children to make ingredients for a magic spell from air-drying clay. If necessary, suggest they could make such things as toads, snake tongues, eyeballs, bat wings and plants. Get them to paint the clay items when dry and arrange them around the cauldron.

Spell books

Put the children into groups of 5 or 6 to make spell books. They can create the outer covers from thick card, then fill their books with pages of spells. For each spell, they should think of an interesting name. They are to list, draw and colour or paint the ingredients, and they can decorate the outer covers with a collage. If they have done the 'Witch's cauldron' activity above, they can include the spell books in their table display.

Find the hidden message

The numbers by the side of each row tell you the letters to write down.
When you have completed the puzzle, look for the message.

	1	2	3	4	5	6
2 4	A	T	J	H	E	K
1 3 5 6	E	N	C	Q	A	T
2 5	D	I	P	F	S	L
1 3 6	B	R	L	O	B	A
2 5	H	C	G	I	K	M

	1	2	3	4	5	6	7	8	9	10	11
2 5 7 10	S	T	O	W	H	I	E	L	K	W	R
3 6 8 11	H	P	I	S	U	T	X	C	M	Z	H
1 4 6 8 11	F	B	T	L	W	E	P	W	Q	J	O
2 5 7 10	Y	U	P	A	T	R	O	G	X	N	C
3 5 9 11	S	M	H	L	E	D	Q	T	R	K	B
1 3 6 8 10	R	Z	O	W	V	O	R	M	F	S	W
2 4 7 9 11	P	T	H	I	N	F	C	D	K	P	O
3 5 8 10	B	Y	N	B	H	I	U	A	M	L	G
1 3 6 8 10 11	L	W	O	Z	C	W	M	E	R	E	N

Now draw a grid and hide a message for someone else to find.

Reach the enchanted castle

A game for two players. Before playing the game, create 32 small cards of equal size and write 4 cards for each of the compass points shown on the diagram. Shuffle the cards and place them face down on the table. Each player needs three counters (each player chooses a different colour). They may place their counters anywhere on the outside shaded area. In turn they pick up a directions card and move one counter in the direction indicated. The first player to get their three counters on the enchanted castle is the winner.

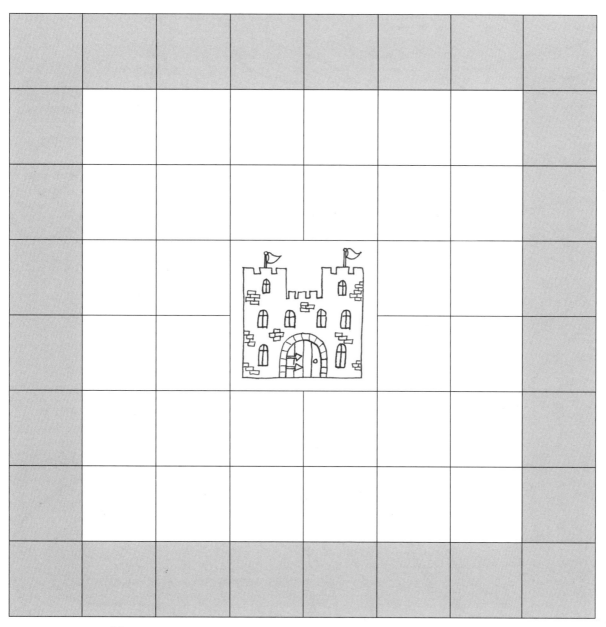

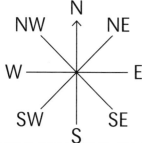

Pathways through the forest

Measure each path with string to see which is the shortest route through the forest.

3.4

The wizard's journey

The wizard's journey through the Land of Magic is plotted on the grid provided. The wizard starts on X at (1.1). Follow the instructions to discover what and whom the wizard meets on the journey. Each time the wizard encounters something new, you will see _____ in the story. Write in the correct item from the list below and its coordinates - for example, glass slipper (5.9) - then cross it off this list:

> cloak, cat, witch, cauldron, glass slipper, broomstick, wand, spell book, potion, ring, fairy, dragon, elf, magic tree.

The wizard begins his journey at (1.1). He goes 4 squares N, then 6 squares E _____ . He continues 5 squares E, then turns and heads N for 5 squares followed by 2 squares E_____. From here he travels 9 squares W and then 1 square S_____. The wizard goes 5 squares S and then 2 W _____. He races 6 squares N, then 6 squares E, before turning S for 2 squares_____. He continues to travel S for 7 squares and then turns E for 5 squares_____. From here he travels 12 squares W, followed by 11 squares N, then 4 squares E_____. He continues to travel E for 5 squares, then turns S for 7 squares_____. He heads N for 8 squares, then W for 7 squares and 2 N_____. From here, he travels 4 squares S, then 2 squares W_____.

Write instructions for the wizard's journey to the four remaining items on the list.

_____

_____

_____

_____

The wizard's journey

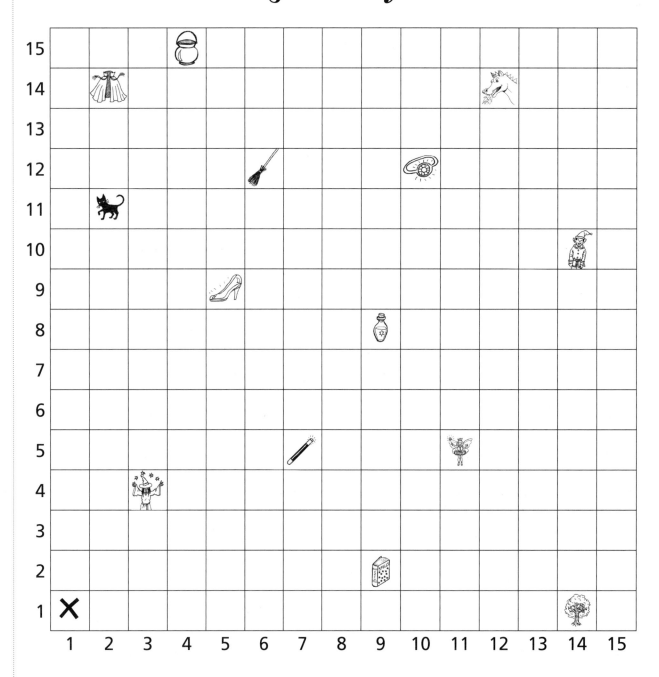

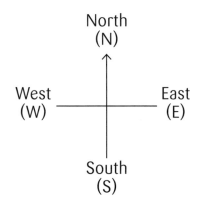

North
(N)

West   East
(W)   (E)

South
(S)

3.6

Complete the magic squares

Complete the small 4 x 4 grid with the four pictures illustrated so that each picture appears in every row, in every column, and in each outlined block of four squares.

If you feel confident, try the 9 x 9 grid, using nine pictures and nine rows, columns and squares.

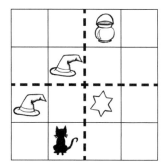

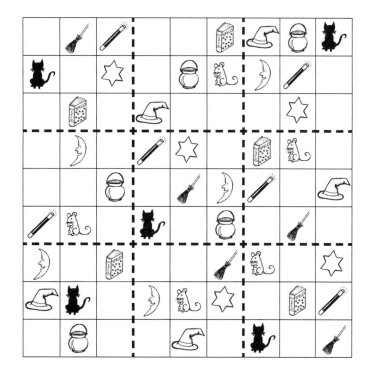

Try making up a puzzle, filling the grid of six squares with your own pictures.

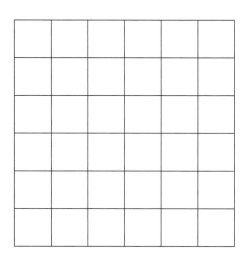

Magic potion

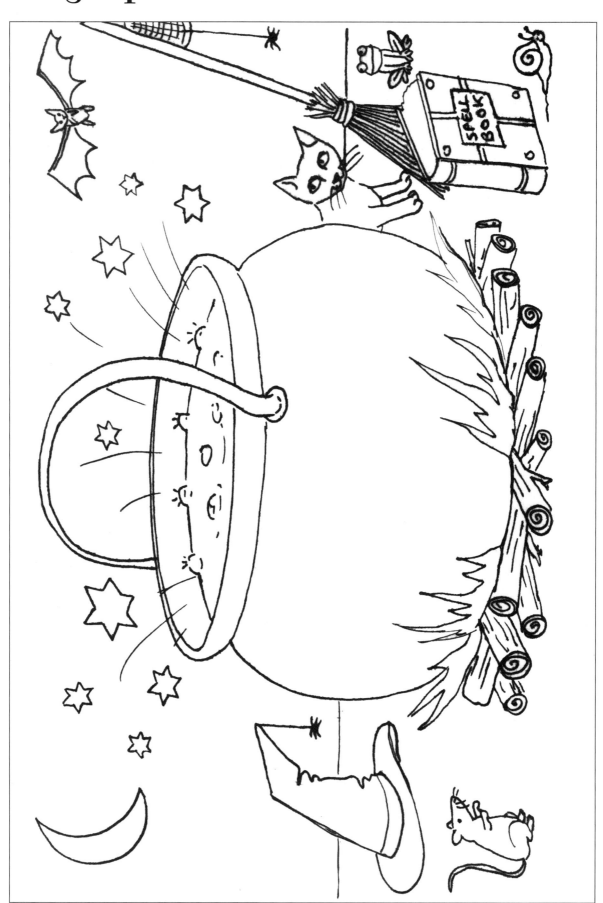

Spot the difference

3.9

Race to the wizard's house

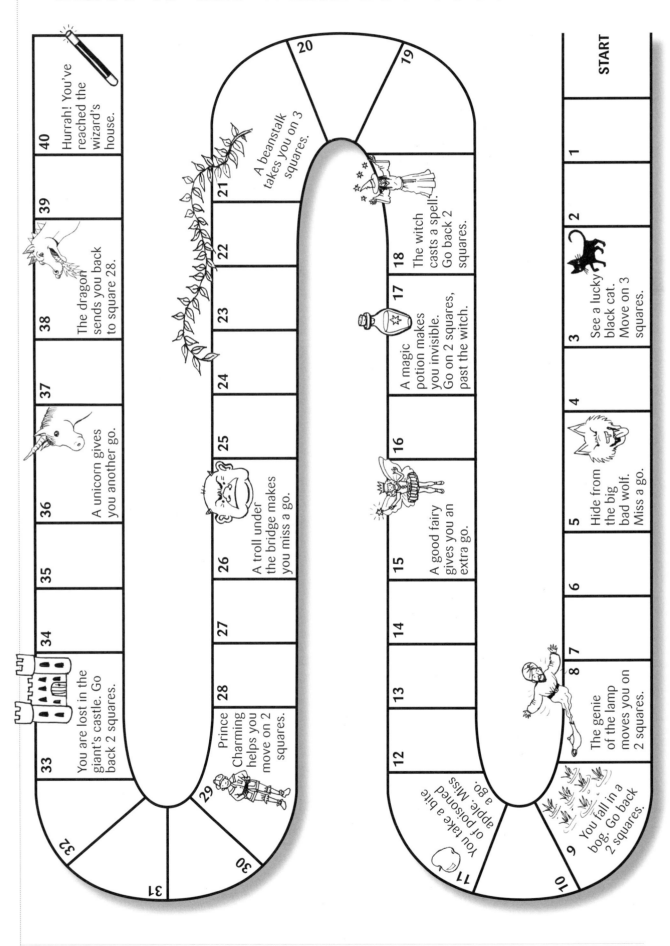

START

1

2 — See a lucky black cat. Move on 3 squares.

3

4

5 — Hide from the big bad wolf. Miss a go.

6

7

8 — The genie of the lamp moves you on 2 squares.

9

10

11 — You take a bite of poisoned apple. Miss a go.

12

13

14

15 — A good fairy gives you an extra go.

16

17 — A magic potion makes you invisible. Go on 2 squares, past the witch.

18 — The witch casts a spell. Go back 2 squares.

19

20

21 — A beanstalk takes you on 3 squares.

22

23

24

25 — A troll under the bridge makes you miss a go.

26

27

28 — Prince Charming helps you move on 2 squares.

29

30

31

32

33 — You are lost in the giant's castle. Go back 2 squares.

34

35

36 — A unicorn gives you another go.

37

38 — The dragon sends you back to square 28.

39

40 — Hurrah! You've reached the wizard's house.

Youssef and the Aztecs

A life or death adventure
in ancient Mexico

Chapter 1

Youssef hadn't really wanted to go to the fair. Most of the rides made him feel sick and he didn't like the hustle and bustle and pushing and jostling of the crowds. He liked to have space around him, but in the end peer pressure prevailed and he went along with his mates.

He had to admit that the bright lights and loud music were infectious, and he enjoyed watching the faces of the people on some of the scarier rides. Eyes tightly shut and mouths wide open, they screamed their way in terror through the five minutes or so of the ride, then staggered on to the next opportunity to be scared witless again.

When his friends opted to go for a particularly terrifying experience, Youssef told them he'd have a little wander around and look at the sights. He bought some candy floss, then sauntered slowly among the stalls and rides. He had a go at hooking a duck, but was unsuccessful, and he fared no better at the shooting gallery. He had reached the outer perimeter of the fairground and was just about to turn back when he noticed a rather small and dimly lit entrance. Above it was a sign announcing 'Aztec Adventure'. It didn't seem to be very popular – Youssef couldn't see anyone either entering or leaving – but he had recently studied the Aztec culture at school and had found it a fascinating subject, so he moved forward for a closer look.

A tall, unsmiling man stood in the doorway, dressed like an Aztec warrior. He had on a long, skirt-like garment covered in geometrical patterns and a feathered headdress. "You want to go in?" he addressed Youssef.

"Mm, I don't know. I don't like rides that make you feel sick," Youssef replied.

"It's not like that, believe me. You'll like it," said the man.

Youssef paid his money and entered through the doorway. He saw a carriage on rails, the sort that you get on ghost trains, and climbed in. The ride took him through a variety of scenes depicting various Aztec customs, including a very realistic human sacrifice with oodles of dripping blood and a fierce-looking priest holding a human heart in his upraised hand. Youssef could see that, thrill-wise, this was a very tame ride compared to the other attractions in the fairground, but he found it enjoyable and fascinating. The life-sized models were very well crafted and the surrounding scenery and artefacts created a really true-to-life impression of being in an Aztec kingdom. Youssef recognised many of the items he had learnt about at school, which added to the overall satisfaction of the ride.

When he emerged through the doorway the attendant asked him, "Well, did you enjoy the ride?"

"Yes, thanks. It was great. It almost felt like I was really there, you know, in Aztec times."

"Would you like to go back and see the real thing, then?" the man asked.

"Wow, you bet!" exclaimed Youssef. "It'd be amazing!"

"Well, as I'm not busy tonight," the man told him, "you can have a free ride and enjoy it all over again."

"That's great, thanks," said Youssef.

It seemed to him that the man gave him a peculiar look as he went back through the door a second time. He wasn't sure why.

Youssef settled into the carriage to enjoy the show again. Having seen all the tableaux once, he was able to pick out more familiar items in each scene. He was glad that he had learnt about Aztec culture, because it meant that he understood what many of the items on display were. For example, he knew that the two interconnected stone circles with designs on them were Aztec calendars, one for the priests and one for farmers, and he recognised some of the gods that were depicted and knew their names.

As the carriage drew to a halt, Youssef pulled himself up from the seat and climbed out. He pushed open the swing door and stepped out into … into what?

It wasn't the fairground. Youssef stopped to take in his surroundings. He was puzzled. It felt hot. The people milling around wore few clothes. He could see square buildings, lots of bright colours and unfamiliar painted symbols. A man walked past him, wearing a brilliant green and red cloak and a long beaded necklace with a heavy and ornate medallion on the end of it. He had bone through his ear and another pierced his nose. Youssef wondered if he had somehow entered another section of the Aztec Adventure, but when he turned round to retrace his steps, the door had vanished.

Glancing down, he saw that his toes were bare and realised that he was now wearing sandals. Examining the rest of his clothes, he was amazed to discover that he was clad in the rich and colourful outfit of an Aztec noble boy.

He seemed to be in a real Aztec community, but how could that have happened? He thought of the conversation he had with the fairground man and remembered the strange look he had given him. Somehow he had travelled back in time to the real thing. He felt scared and excited at the same time. Taking a deep breath, he strode forward into the crowd of milling people. He didn't know where he was going, but he intended to have a good look round while he had the opportunity.

Chapter 2

Because Youssef appeared to be a boy of noble birth, he was treated with deference by all the commoners he passed. They nodded to him and moved out of his way. He passed through a busy, crowded market and looked around at the colourful stalls. There were fresh, glowing fruit and vegetables – tomatoes, maize cobs, chilli peppers, sweet peppers, avocado pears, pineapples and pumpkins. Other stalls displayed gold jewellery, beautiful cloaks and headdresses made from featherwork. There was even a section selling live animals such as snakes and monkeys. It was exciting and noisy.

Youssef worked out that he was in the Aztec capital, Tenochtitlan. There were images of gods that he remembered from his school project. Quetzalcoatl, represented by a feathered serpent, was the god of learning, hope and healing. Huitzilzopochtli, represented by a blue humming bird, was the god who was the patron of war. Then there was Coyolxauhqui, the goddess of the moon, and Tezcatlipoca, the god of human sacrifice. Seeing the last of these made Youssef shiver at the grim thought of all the human victims that had fallen prey to the Aztecs' gruesome practices.

The strange thing was that, as he walked along, Youssef suddenly realised that he could understand what everyone was saying, even though they were talking in a foreign language. This ability was obviously a feature of the time-travel, as were the clothes he was wearing.

He stopped to listen to a storyteller entertaining a group of children. The storyteller was reading from an Aztec book called a codex – Youssef remembered that the plural of this word was codices. Unlike books at home, a codex was made from a long strip of paper that was folded like a concertina. The paper was made by soaking the bark of fig trees in water containing limestone to soften the fibres. They were then beaten, glued together with resin and flattened into a thin sheet. The codex did not contain writing as the Aztecs did not have a written language, but the pages were covered in bright, colourful drawings called glyphs. The outline of the glyphs was drawn with a pointed stick and ink made from soot. They were then coloured using pigments made from plants. If they wrote about something like a god, they would draw a bigger picture to emphasise its importance. Although the story about the god Quetzalcoatl was very entertaining, Youssef thought he had better continue the investigation of his surroundings.

As he walked along, he saw a weeping child being held over a fire of smouldering chilli peppers by an angry-looking adult. "He's obviously done something naughty," thought Youssef, remembering that this was a form of punishment Aztec parents used. The rising fumes from the burning chilli peppers stung and irritated the victim's eyes.

"Gosh," he thought, "I'm glad my mum doesn't do that to me when I do something wrong."

Walking on further, Youssef arrived in an area with grander-looking buildings of two or more storeys. He walked up the front steps and through the doorway of one of the buildings, entering a central courtyard in which there were a pond and a garden filled with bright flowers. Feeling hot and thirsty, he sat down by the pond. A man who was obviously a servant approached Youssef to ask if he required anything. Youssef asked for a drink and discovered that the servant could understand him. It was amazing!

The servant disappeared into one of the rooms and reappeared some minutes later carrying a beaker that he offered to Youssef. It contained a frothing chocolate drink that was absolutely delicious. Feeling somewhat peckish, Youssef decided to ask for food as well, and soon he was wolfing down a tortilla filled with spicy vegetables and some kind of strange meat. He wished he hadn't asked the servant what the meat was when he discovered it was frog, but by that time he had already finished the tasty meal.

Feeling refreshed and satisfied, Youssef decided to continue his journey through the city. Ahead of him he could see the Great Temple, a huge stepped pyramid that he remembered had been built in line with two sacred volcanoes nearby. There were shrines on its summit to both the rain god, Tlaloc, and the god of war, Huitzilopochtli. When the Spanish had conquered the Aztecs, Youssef remembered, they had destroyed most of their frightening images of gods and the temples, so it was good to see them as they had originally been, in all their glory.

As Youssef walked on towards the Great Temple, he became aware of someone crying. Looking around, he saw a woman peering at the temple from behind a building. Tears streamed down her face as she wept openly. Youssef approached the woman and asked her what the matter was. She was ordinary and rather poor looking, and she appeared to be taken aback and a little frightened at being addressed by a noble person. However, when Youssef repeated his question she stopped crying and answered him.

"I am a widow and my only son was captured in the Flowery War. He is to be sacrificed tomorrow and his heart will be given as an offering to the god. I love him very much and I don't know how I will manage without him."

Youssef was dismayed by the poor woman's anguish and wondered if he could do anything to help. "Tell me the name of your son," he said to her, "and I'll see if there is anything I can do to save him."

Youssef didn't have a plan, but he seemed to be able to go anywhere in his fine clothes. It was worth a try to see if he could somehow help to reunite the weeping woman with her son.

Chapter 3

Youssef tried to remember what he had learnt about the Flowery Wars of the Aztecs. They sounded charming, as if warriors threw flowers at one another, but in fact the flower connection was made because the warriors fell in battle like a shower of blossoms. They were anything but charming.

The Aztecs had used the flowery wars against neighbouring tribes to take captives for sacrifice. They were a gruesome lot. As well as ripping out hearts, they sacrificed people to the god of water, Tlaloc, by throwing them into a lake. Also, they skinned people alive.

Youssef decided to get nearer to the temple to see what he could find out. He knew the woman's son was called Tizoc. He thought that perhaps, as a noble boy, he could gain access to him and find a way of releasing him. Telling the woman to remain where she was and wait for him to return, he set off down the road in the direction of the Great Temple.

In the centre of a largish square, a 70m-high post reared up into the air. Looking upwards, Youssef could see a group of young men standing on a platform. One of them was playing a flute and the others were busily tying ropes to their bodies.

"Oh, it's the holy birdman game," Youssef thought. "I must stop and watch this. It's just like bungee jumping."

As he gazed upwards, the young men, who were dressed in feathered costumes and bird masks, threw themselves from the platform while the flautist played a lively tune. The birds swung around thirteen times before they touched down on the ground.

It was quite breathtaking, but not something that Youssef wanted to try. It reminded him too much of the scary fairground rides.

Youssef continued to walk towards the Great Temple. He encountered some priests along the way and had to hold his nose as they passed by. Their grimy clothes were covered in soot and dried blood, and smelled appalling. Also, because they weren't allowed to cut or wash their hair, it was sticking out in all directions and was covered in buzzing insects. They had drops of blood running down their necks, so Youssef knew that they had been pricking their ears with cactus spines so that they could offer drops of their own blood to appease the gods. Even ordinary people started their day with this ritual. Youssef was really glad that he hadn't been born an Aztec so that he would have to prick his own body with cactus spines.

Approaching the Great Temple, Youssef shielded his eyes against the sun and gazed upwards at its magnificent height. It was 60m tall with dozens of steps rising up to its summit, which was where the human sacrifices took place. The temple walls were decorated with beautiful paintings of gods and ancestors in vivid colours.

Youssef's next encounter was somewhat less attractive. A huge rack of grinning skulls piled one on top of the other caught his eye. Averting his gaze, he hurried past. He needed to find out where the prisoners were being held.

By listening to conversations taking place around him, Youssef gleaned that the Aztecs were planning a great festival called the New Fire Ceremony. This took place only once every 52 years, when the priests' calendar and the farmers' calendar ended on the same day. The priests' calendar had 13 months, each divided into 20 days, whereas the farmers' calendar had 360 days plus 5 extra unlucky ones. All the lights and fires in the city were put out. After five days the priests would make their sacrifices and new fires could be lit.

After more listening in, Youssef discovered the whereabouts of the captive prisoners and set off to try to find Tizoc. He approached the prison entrance fearfully, worried that he might end up with the same fate as the captured men, but it seemed that his noble appearance gave him the freedom to do just about anything he wanted. The guards simply nodded to him by way of greeting and he walked past them without further ado.

The prisoners were confined in wooden crates and there seemed to be hundreds of them. However was he going to find the woman's son among so many? Nevertheless, he set to work. Walking among the crates, he stopped at each one asking if there was anyone called Tizoc. One 'Yes' came from an oldish man, and Youssef dismissed him. Another 'Yes' looked promising as it came from a young man, but further questioning revealed that this Tizoc had several brothers as well as both parents. Eventually, however, Youssef thought he had found the right person. He asked for a description of the young man's mother and it matched the woman he had spoken to.

Youssef beckoned Tizoc to the edge of the crate and whispered in his ear. "I am planning to return tonight, when everyone is asleep, and try to release you. I have spoken to your mother and she will be waiting for you in a safe hiding-place."

Tizoc looked at Youssef with deep suspicion, so Youssef added, "Don't be deceived by my clothes. I am in disguise. I am not an Aztec, I am from another place."

Saying goodbye, he walked out of the prison. He needed to work out exactly what he would do later on. Everything rested on his thinking of a fool-proof plan. It was a life or death situation!

Chapter 4

The first thing that Youssef did when he left the prison was to find Tizoc's mother. He told her that he intended to return that night and try to find a way of releasing her son. The poor woman wept with gratitude and blessed Youssef by all the gods she could think of.

The problem was that, in spite of his assurances to Tizoc's mother, Youssef did not have the faintest idea how he was going to keep his promise to her. He needed a plan. He found a shady spot beneath a tree and sat down to think.

The one thing that Youssef had noticed time and time again was how the common people deferred to the noble classes. Because he had the appearance of nobility, this might work in his favour. He thought back to his encounter with the servant in the wealthy household he had visited and wondered why his identity had not been questioned. The servant had simply carried out his demands without asking him once who he was or what he was doing in the house. Perhaps it was because servants never questioned the nobility, or perhaps it was just part of the magic that had taken him back to Aztec times in the first place. Slowly a plan began to formulate in his mind. It depended very heavily on the prison guard also respecting his noble birth, but it was all he could think of.

The first part of the plan required him to return to the house he had previously visited. Once again, the servant appeared and enquired if he needed anything. Youssef asked for a fresh change of clothes and some food. When these had been delivered, Youssef used the new cloak to wrap up some of the food. He made a neat bundle of the rest, using the cloth the servant had brought to serve the food on. Then, just in case the servant reappeared, he made a hasty exit.

He would not return to the prison until some time during the night when everyone else was asleep, so he had several hours to fill. He found a safe hiding-place for his bundle, then wandered about the city, taking in the sights. There was plenty to see and enjoy on the crowded streets.

Gradually the streets began to clear as people drifted off to their homes and beds. Youssef was glad of his warm cloak as the temperature dipped and the air became chilly. After a couple more hours, he decided the time was right. Everywhere the streets lay deserted apart from a stray dog, rummaging among the rubbish in search of scraps of food.

Youssef made his way back to the prison. The young guard on the door looked him up and down, but made no attempt to detain him. Once inside, Youssef inspected his surroundings. Everyone appeared to be asleep – the stillness was punctuated by the rumbling snores of all the sleepers, both guards and prisoners. Youssef would need the assistance of a guard to unlock the wooden crate that Tizoc lay in, but which one should he choose? Looking around, he decided on the oldest guard, who seemed to be in the deepest sleep, and gently roused him.

"Er, yes. What do you want?" the guard asked groggily, staggering to his feet and blinking wearily.

"I've been sent by my father to bring back the prisoner Tizoc," Youssef told him.

"Why?" asked the guard.

"My father did not tell me. He just said it was urgent," Youssef replied.

The guard looked at him suspiciously. Now was the time for Youssef to make use of his noble appearance. "Do you know who I am?" he demanded. "One word from me and you will find yourself taking Tizoc's place along with the other prisoners. Do you want to be a human sacrifice as well?"

The guard suddenly looked terrified. He certainly did not want to share the prisoners' fate. He decided that one young man among the dozens they had captured would not be missed anyway, and asked Youssef to show him the prisoner that he required. The boy led him through the maze of wooden crates until he found the one he was looking for. Kneeling down, he poked Tizoc through the bars of the cage. When the young man raised a sleepy head, Youssef gestured with a finger to his lips, telling him to be silent. The guard unlocked the cage and Tizoc crept out. Without a backward glance, Youssef led the released prisoner out on to the street, breathing a huge sigh of relief as the door closed behind them.

The next part of the plan was to wrap Tizoc in the cloak that Youssef had brought with him, give him something to eat, and then set out together to retrieve the hidden bundle. As two young nobles, they should be left alone to make good their escape. Even if anyone was suspicious about what they were doing wandering the streets in the middle of the night, they were unlikely to question them.

The two made their way stealthily along, keeping close to the buildings. Youssef guided Tizoc to the place where his mother waited, anxiously peering out from her hiding-place. When she saw the two approaching figures, she leapt out and rushed forwards to embrace her son. Tears of joy streamed down her beaming face as she hugged Tizoc and repeated her thanks for his return to Youssef.

"We must leave this place quickly," Tizoc urged his mother, "or I will be recaptured." He turned to Youssef and said, "You told me that you are not an Aztec. Where are you from, then?"

"That's a rather difficult question to answer," Youssef told him. "I don't think you would believe me if I told you. Let's just say that the gods sent me to rescue you."

"In that case," said Tizoc, "you had better return to our home with us."

Chapter 5

The three figures made their way carefully and quietly through the city. Even dressed as nobles, Youssef did not want to risk arousing suspicion and having to answer unwelcome questions. As they left the last of the buildings behind them, they all let out a huge sigh of relief – they were free! However, there was still a long way to go. The path was through desert, where they might encounter wild animals, snakes and scorpions, and there would be scorching heat during the day and cold nights.

Luckily they had provisions for the journey as Youssef had the bundle of food and Tizoc's mother had filled her water container before they had left.

They trudged on through the night. In the moonlight the giant cacti looked like menacing warriors with their arms raised ready for battle. To pass the time, Tizoc told Youssef about his town and family. It was not as large or wealthy as the Aztec city and the people who lived there were in constant fear of their warlike neighbours. The community had to pay an annual tax to the Aztecs of 20 warrior outfits, 400 fine cloaks, 40 shields, 400 boxes of cotton, 20 boxes of beans and 400 baskets of chilli peppers. This was a heavy burden and it kept the people who lived in Tizoc's town in poverty.

His father had been killed in a tragic accident, so it was up to Tizoc to provide for his mother and himself. He was able to earn some money by making items for rich people as he was a skilled feather-worker who could create beautiful and delicate patterns that were much in demand. His mother tended their vegetable plot, and so they were able to survive. It would have been a devastating blow for her to lose her son and only source of income.

The pair did not stop thanking Youssef, and they were very intrigued by his origins. He knew they wouldn't believe the truth, so he merely told them that he had travelled from a very distant place.

Slowly the dark sky took on a paler tinge and the sun appeared over the horizon. The three walkers were glad the chilly night was over and looked forward to feeling the warm rays of the sun on them.

They stopped to eat, drink and take a rest, and felt greatly refreshed after their meal. They continued the journey throughout the intense heat of the day, and as the sun dipped in the sky they reached their destination, hungry and weary.

Before entering their town, Tizoc suggested that he and Youssef should remove their fine Aztec clothes. "It would be a pity to have escaped the Aztecs only to be killed by my own people in a case of mistaken identity," he laughingly told Youssef.

He led him to his home, a simple hut made with wattle walls, its roof thatched with maguey cactus leaves. Inside it was very bare, with just a couple of bedding mats and straw cushions to sit on.

Tizoc's mother prepared and cooked them a meal which made Youssef feel so much better. Having eaten, he decided to take a walk around the town. The buildings and inhabitants were obviously poor and Youssef thought it was very unfair of their stronger neighbours to treat them so harshly. He began to think of his own circumstances, and for the first time started to worry about his predicament.

Here he was trapped in time, away from friends and family. What was going to happen to him? Would he ever see his own home again? He sat down on a low wall to think, feeling sad and anxious.

"Excuse me, are you lost?" enquired a voice.

Looking up, Tizoc saw a man who seemed familiar, but he couldn't quite remember from where.

"I think I can help you. Follow me," the man told him.

Before he could ask any questions, the man set off along the street. Youssef had no other plan, so he stood up and followed the disappearing figure. The man led the way towards a large building that Youssef thought must be a temple. By the time he reached the entrance, the man had already vanished inside.

"I hope this isn't some kind of deadly trap," thought Youssef, as he plunged in through the doorway.

He saw the man walking through another doorway at the opposite end of the building and quickened his pace to try to catch up with him. As he emerged from the building, the familiar sights, sounds and smells of the fairground greeted him. Youssef suddenly remembered where he had seen the man's face before – he was the fairground attendant who had offered him the ride in the first place. Now he was nowhere to be seen.

A scruffy man in jeans and T-shirt stood by the entrance.

"Excuse me," Youssef said to him. "Where's the other attendant? You know, the one dressed as an Aztec."

The man looked at him as though he were mad.

"He was here earlier," Youssef told him. "He took my money."

"You must be having a hallucination, mate," the man told him. "There's no one like that here."

When Youssef caught up with his friends, they told him they'd been searching for him for ages. "What have you been doing, anyway?" they asked him.

"Oh, nothing much," Youssef told them. He decided it must all have been some kind of waking dream.

That night, as he took his clothes off two bright green feathers fluttered to the floor.

Follow-up work for each chapter

CHAPTER 1

Tell the children to imagine that they have travelled forwards or backwards in time. Where have they landed? Ask them to either write about where they are, whether it is in the past or the future, who lives there and what is happening; or draw and label a picture showing these details.

CHAPTER 2

The Aztecs used pictograms or glyphs instead of writing. Ask the children to think up picture representations for the following:

> dog, house, child, mother, father, bed, dinner, drink, rain, wind, warrior, rich, poor, happy.

Tell them to think of some words of their own to represent in picture form. Get them to see if they can write a sentence using their pictures (tell them not to worry about a picture form for joining words such as 'and' and 'in').

CHAPTER 3

Ask the children to imagine that they are involved in a flowery war. They can either be an Aztec warrior who is victorious in the battle and captures a prisoner, or a warrior from the opposing side who is captured. Tell them to write an account of the battle or draw a comic strip of the event. Encourage them to think of as many details as they can, such as what the warriors wore (animal masks, feathered garments, etc.) and what they carried (spears, shields, bows and arrows, etc.). If they have time, they could describe the events that happened after the battle, when they returned to the Aztec city.

CHAPTER 4

Ask the children to make up some triangular poems about the Aztecs, in five lines. In the first line there is one word, in the second two and so on up to the fifth line, where there are five words. Here is an example:

The

Aztecs liked

To eat spicy

Chilli peppers and lots

Of different vegetables in tortillas.

CHAPTER 5

Tell the children that they are going to use the Aztec face on the Things that I like template, 4.1 (p. 96), to record things that they like. For each item they are to record the number of things on the worksheet (e.g. 3 things I like to listen to, 5 things I like to eat). Let the children compare their choices with their friends. They could discuss how many things they had in common.

Ideas for maths work

Aztec maths

Give each child a copy of the Aztec maths template, 4.2 (p. 97). Instructions for using the symbols are on the sheet.

Aztec dinners

The children should work in groups of 6 to 8, each seated at a table. Each group has a copy of the Aztec dinners template, 4.3 (p. 98). They use it to plan a meal and work out what it costs.

Aztec shields

This game is played in pairs, with one copy of the Aztec shields template, 4.4 (p. 99), for each pair. Instructions are given on the sheet.

Aztec mazes

Give each child a copy of the Aztec mazes template, 4.5 (p. 100). When they have completed the two mazes, they can try devising their own.

Journey through the desert

Each child has a copy of the Journey through the desert template, 4.6 (p. 101). The activity is in two parts, giving those who complete the first quickly the opportunity to try a more difficult version.

Science activities

Volcanoes

Volcanoes were very special to the Aztecs. Tell the children that they may do their own experiment to show what a volcano looks like when it erupts. In pairs, or small groups, the children make a volcano. First they colour a yoghurt pot or polystyrene cup brown and make a large hole in the base. (It may be a good idea to reduce the height of the pot to about 5 cm.) They place the inverted pot over a mound of bicarbonate of soda. Next they prepare a mixture of vinegar and red food colouring. Then they trickle some of this liquid through the hole in the base of the pot on to the bicarbonate of soda. A chemical reaction occurs, causing the mixture to bubble up through the hole, like lava. You can extend this experiment by asking the children to create a scene for their volcano (e.g. with grass and trees) and photograph the eruptions.

Balloon blowing

If you are using bicarbonate of soda and vinegar, you can ask the children to carry out a further experiment. They will need bottles with narrow necks and balloons.

They pour vinegar into their bottle until it is a quarter full, then use a funnel to pour bicarbonate of soda into the deflated balloon. Next they carefully stretch the neck of the balloon over the bottle opening, keeping the balloon to one side so that no bicarbonate of soda falls into the bottle. Once the balloon is in place, it can be upended so that the powder falls on to the vinegar. Warn the children to stand some distance from the balloon in case it bursts. A chemical reaction takes place (as with the volcanoes) and carbon dioxide is released that will inflate the balloon.

Other activities

Aztec warrior

Copy template 4.7 (p. 102) to make a copy for each child. Encourage them to complete and colour the border, then colour in the picture.

Aztec calendar

The children create symbols for months of the year and special days. Each needs a copy of the Aztec calendar template, 4.8 (p. 103).

Where's the spear?

Put the children in pairs. Give each pair a copy of template 4.9 (p. 104), and a different number. Instructions are given on the sheet.

Aztec figure

Give each child a copy of the Aztec figure template, 4.10 (p. 105). Explain that they are to make a copy of the Aztec figure on the small grid, square by square, on to the big grid.

Aztec fishermen

The children work individually, each with their own copy of the Aztec fishermen template, 4.11 (p. 106).

Active games

Aztec warrior relay

Put the children into teams of 6. Prior to the lesson, each team will need to make or collect the following:

- length of material to make a wrap-around skirt, and string for tying round the waist
- length of material to make a cloak, and a means of fastening it
- headdress (give each group a copy of template 4.12, p. 107, and see the instructions on p. 95 [Animal headdress])

- shield (see template 4.13, p. 108)
- spear (bamboo cane or broom handle).

One child in each team is the Aztec warrior, to be dressed by their team-mates. The items are placed at one end of the room (or playground) and the teams line up at the opposite end. One at a time, the team members race to the far end of the room, collect an item and bring it back for their warrior. The items must be collected in the order listed above. Each item must be fitted properly on to the warrior (e.g. the skirt must be secured with string, the cloak fastened) before the next team member may go. The winner is the first team to have fully dressed their warrior and all be seated on the ground.

Catch the monkey's tail

Every child needs a length of material to tuck into their waist-band at the back and represent a monkey's tail. Each tail should have around 20cm on show.

The object of the game is for the children to try to capture tails from other monkeys, while retaining their own tails. Once their own tail is captured, they are out and they sit on the sidelines. When all the tails are captured or the children are exhausted, count up the captured tails to see who is the champion monkey.

Hot chilli pepper

The children stand in a large circle. A bean-bag or soft ball represents a hot chilli pepper. One child begins the action by calling the name of another in the circle, then throwing the chilli pepper to them. The first child then sits down. The action continues this way with the chilli pepper being thrown from child to child, and the thrower then sitting down. When you are left with one child standing holding the chilli pepper, this child sits down as well. Remind the children to call the name before throwing the bean-bag and to throw sensibly to avoid accidents. If you time the game, you can repeat the activity several times to see if the children can improve their time.

Flowery war

You will need a large soft ball for this game. Choose four children to be Aztec warriors. They can pass the ball between themselves, but cannot move. The remaining children are another tribe and may move freely around the room. The object of the game is for the Aztec warriors to hit members of the other tribe with the ball. If they succeed, those they hit are stuck to the ground and must help the warriors. The game continues until all the tribe have been conquered or the children are tiring.

Aztec assault

Choose three children to be Aztec warriors. They stand at one end of the room, facing the wall. The remaining children slowly creep up on them and try to touch them before they turn round. When the Aztec warriors turn round, they chase the other children back to their starting point and anyone they tag is out. If someone successfully touches a warrior they take their place. Allow several goes, then choose new warriors.

Art

Animal headdress

Explain to the children that they are going to create animal headdresses and show them the examples on template 4.12 (p. 107) – provide enough copies for them to use. They must make sure that they make them large enough to fit their heads. They draw one side on card or sugar paper, then cut that out. They use the cut-out as a template for the second side to make sure that both sides match. They then colour in their headdresses. Tell them to cut out several card strips 3 cm wide. The sides are attached to each other by stapling the front together at the top and bottom, to create a window that the children can look through. They use several card strips at intervals to join the headdress at the top and back.

Aztec shields

Make a few photocopies of template 4.13 (p. 108) to distribute among the children. Create a large circle of stiff card for each child. Explain that they are going to create their own Aztec shield in bright colours. Show them the examples of designs on the template. They can create feathers or use real ones if you have any available to add to their shields. When the shields are finished, have the children put on their animal masks, hold their shield and stand together in war-like poses for a photograph.

Aztec pots

Tell the children they are going to make coil pots; see illustrations below. They should roll out their clay into ropes and make a base (diagram 1), then build up the sides of the pot (diagram 2). When the clay is dry, they can paint a design on their pots.

1

2

Things that I like

3 things I am good at are:

_____

_____

_____

The part of my body I like
best is:

_____

3 things I like to look at are:

_____

_____

_____

3 things I like the smell of are:

_____

_____

_____

5 things I like to eat are:

_____

_____

_____

_____

_____

3 things I like to
listen to are:

_____

_____

_____

Aztec maths

Look at the value for each symbol and work out what the numbers in section 1 are.
If you can manage those, go on to the sums in sections 2 and 3.
Ask your teacher or teaching assistant if you need help with section 1.

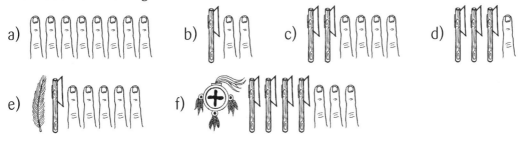

= 1   = 20   = 400   = 800
finger   knife   feather   shield

1. Work out the following numbers:

   a)   b)   c)   d)

   e)   f)

2. Try these sums. Give your answers in Aztec symbols.

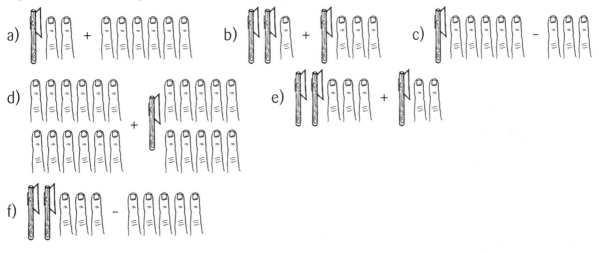

   a)   +   b)   +   c)   −

   d)   +   e)   +

   f)   −

3. Now try these.

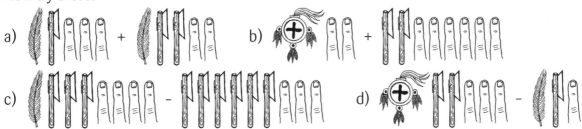

   a)   +   b)   +

   c)   −   d)   −

4. Invent Aztec symbols for 5, 50 and 100. Make up sums of your own using Aztec symbols
   and your invented symbols.

Aztec dinners

Ask everyone, in turn, on your table what they would like to eat from the menu below.
Work out how many cocoa beans each meal will cost. When you have finished,
try to work out the total cost for your table.

tortilla	5 beans OOOOO	fish	18 beans OOOOO OOOOO OOOOO OOO
tomato	3 beans OOO	lettuce	6 beans OOOOO O
maize cob	7 beans OOOOO OO	chocolate drink	35 beans OOOOOOOOOO OOOOOOOOOO OOOOOOOOOO OOOOO
chilli pepper	4 beans OOOO	fruit juice	12 beans OOOOO OOOOO OO
sweet pepper	6 beans OOOOO O	peanuts	10 beans OOOOO OOOOO
deer meat	15 beans OOOOO OOOOO OOOOO	avocado	8 beans OOOOO OOO
turkey meat	23 beans OOOOOOOOOO OOOOOOOOOO OOO	pineapple	12 beans OOOOO OOOOO OO

Aztec shields

Play this maths game with a partner. You will each need a different-coloured set of
ten counters and two dice. Throw the dice and add the total of the numbers shown.
Put your counter on a shield with the same number. Once a shield has a counter,
it can't be used again. The first player to place all ten counters is the winner.

Permission to Photocopy

Aztec mazes

Find your way through the Aztec mazes. Start with the smallest one first.

Try drawing a maze for a friend to get through.

Start →
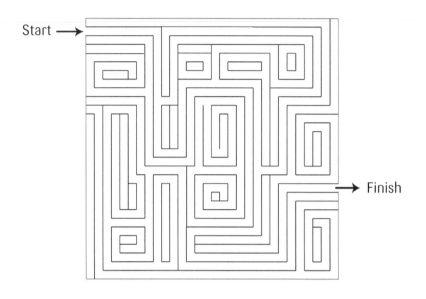
→ Finish

Start →
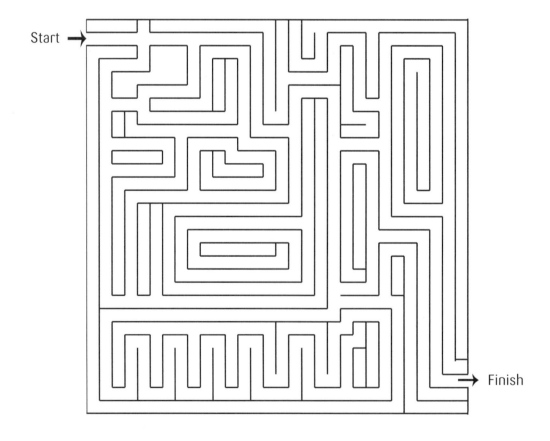
→ Finish

Journey through the desert

How long does the journey through the desert take?
Add up all the separate times and put the answer at the end.
Start with the instructions for journey a). If you have time, go on to journey b).

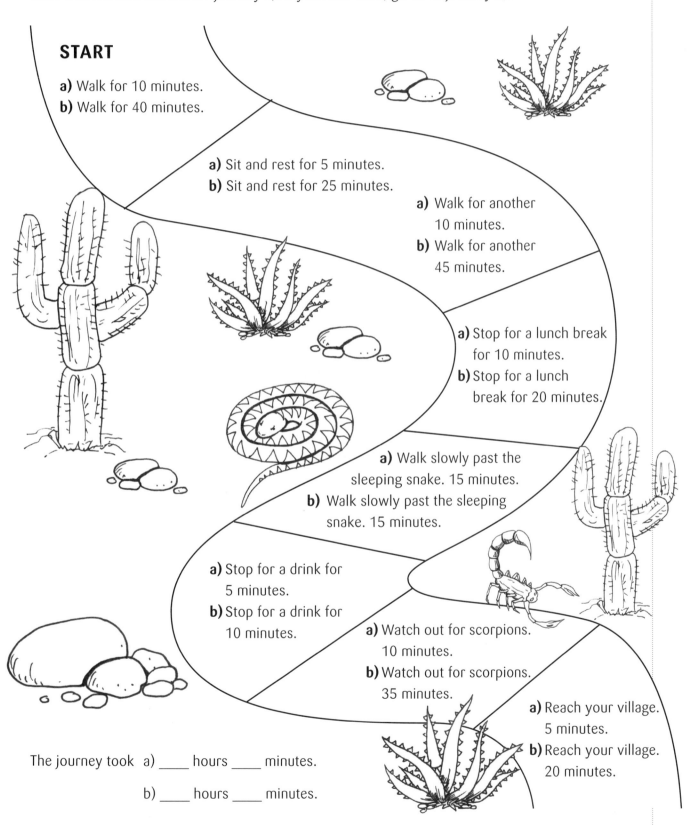

START

a) Walk for 10 minutes.
b) Walk for 40 minutes.

a) Sit and rest for 5 minutes.
b) Sit and rest for 25 minutes.

a) Walk for another 10 minutes.
b) Walk for another 45 minutes.

a) Stop for a lunch break for 10 minutes.
b) Stop for a lunch break for 20 minutes.

a) Walk slowly past the sleeping snake. 15 minutes.
b) Walk slowly past the sleeping snake. 15 minutes.

a) Stop for a drink for 5 minutes.
b) Stop for a drink for 10 minutes.

a) Watch out for scorpions. 10 minutes.
b) Watch out for scorpions. 35 minutes.

a) Reach your village. 5 minutes.
b) Reach your village. 20 minutes.

The journey took a) ____ hours ____ minutes.

b) ____ hours ____ minutes.

Aztec warrior

Complete and colour the border, then colour in the picture.

4.8

Aztec calendar

Below are some symbols from the Aztec calendar. Make up your own symbols for the months of the year and for special days. Choose your own day for the blank space.

grass	water	dog	flower	rain	wind	house

January	February	March	April
May	June	July	August
September	October	November	December
Your birthday	Christmas Day	Easter Monday	

Where's the spear?

In pairs, design and colour the shields. With your partner, secretly decide which shield you will hide your spear behind and make a small mark on the back of the paper to show which it is. Go round the room with your sheet and ask each pair to guess which shield is their choice, then write the number of each pair beside the shield they guess. At the end take turns to say which pair(s) guessed correctly.

Aztec figure

Copy the figure on the small grid,
square by square, on to the big grid
to create a big Aztec figure.

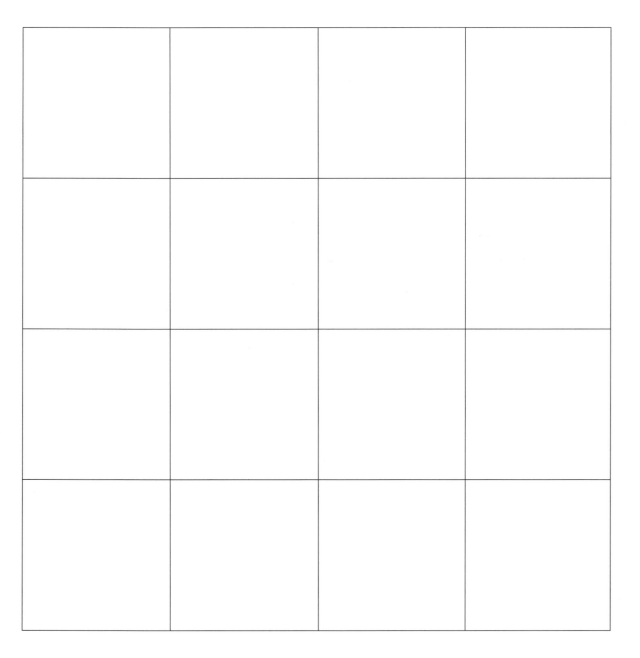

Aztec fishermen

Which of the Aztec fisherman has caught the fish? When you have found out, colour the fish. Using just three colours, can you colour each fish in a different way?

Animal headdress

Aztec shields

Amina and the Flying Carpet

A tale of exotic places around the world

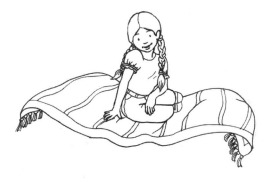

Chapter 1

Amina was the youngest of five children. She lived with her parents, three brothers and sister in a house that never seemed quite big enough for so many people. In this busy household Amina was left to amuse herself much of the time, and had developed a passion for reading. She enjoyed all books, but particularly loved reading about other countries. She liked to learn about the traditions and customs of foreign people, what sort of houses they lived in, what kind of food they ate. She was enthralled by some of the strange animals and exotic birds she saw in the pages of her books and would have loved to be able to see them in real life. Most days, after school, Amina could be found on her bed, lost in another world of exciting places seen through the pages of a book.

One Saturday, at the start of her half-term holiday, Amina's mother called her to go into town. She wanted Amina's advice on a new rug that she intended to purchase for the lounge. The room had been newly decorated and Amina's mum thought that a bright rug would add the finishing touch. Reluctantly, Amina put down her book and clattered down the stairs. She would much rather stay at home reading, but she didn't want to disappoint her mother.

At the carpet shop, Amina was amazed by the number and variety of rugs on display. Lining the walls and spread over most of the floor, they provided a riot of pattern and colour. Her mother began the serious business of searching for the ideal rug to enhance her lounge, so Amina turned to the salesman to pursue her own line of interest.

"Do you have any rugs from Turkey?" she asked him. "I'm reading a book about Turkey and I know that it is famous for the rugs made there."

"Why, yes, indeed," the man answered. "Follow me." He led Amina to a section of the showroom and indicated a collection of rugs on the floor. "These are all Turkish," he told her.

Amina admired the vibrant colours and beautiful designs. "They're so beautiful," she said to the salesman. "I would love to go and see where they're made."

"Are you interested in Turkey, then?" asked the man.

"I'm interested in all countries, "Amina told him. "I spend all my spare time reading about other places and wishing I could visit them."

"I might have just the thing for you," the man remarked. He disappeared through a door and emerged a few minutes later, carrying a bundle under his arm. Reaching Amina, he removed the bundle and unrolled it to display a small oblong carpet. The carpet had a central design of the world, surrounded by animals from various countries. There was a tiger from India, an elephant from Africa, a giant panda from China and a polar bear from the Arctic Circle.

"This is just the thing to sit on when you are reading about other countries. It will help to stimulate your imagination," said the man.

"Oh, I don't think my mother would buy that for me," Amina replied.

"It's not for sale," the man told her. "I'm going to let you borrow it for one week. Unfortunately, you can't keep it as there is a great demand for such a carpet and I only have this one. I will need it back for others to enjoy, but I am sure it will bring you great pleasure."

Amina thought it was all a bit strange, borrowing a carpet for just a week, but her mother seemed quite happy with the arrangement and it would be nice to sit on the carpet and look at all the animals while she was reading. Amina agreed with her mother's choice of rug for the lounge and, once all the paperwork had been completed, they left the shop to return home. Amina, clutching the small carpet under her arm, was impatient to get back to her book so she declined her mother's offer of a drink and a cake in the local café.

When she was back in her bedroom, she rolled out the carpet on the floor, collected her book and sat cross-legged on the map of the world. While she was reading, she glanced from time to time at the pictures woven around her. The animals were beautifully crafted and looked almost realistic, if in miniature.

Glancing at a leaping kangaroo, she said aloud to herself, "I'd love to jump alongside a kangaroo."

Amina felt a strange, wobbling sensation beneath her and the carpet lifted itself up and hovered a metre above the bedroom floor. Amina shrieked and clutched the sides in terror, wondering what on earth was going on. She thought back to what the man in the carpet shop had told her, and suddenly the truth hit her.

"Oh, my gosh," she shrieked. "It's a flying carpet!" As she began to laugh, the carpet rose higher into the air, then whizzed through the open window and up into the sky.

Amina had read about flying carpets in plenty of her story books and knew that they were good things. Her initial apprehension gave way to excitement and she decided to relax and enjoy the journey.

She looked down to watch a changing landscape of fields, rivers, seas, deserts and mountains beneath her. Although they seemed to be covering great distances, it was happening very quickly. After some time the carpet appeared to be slowing down. The landscape now was dusty and brown and Amina could see blurred movement ahead of her in the distance. As they got nearer, Amina gasped with joy. A group of twenty or so kangaroos was bouncing along at a fair speed. The carpet descended until it was in the middle of the group of animals and then kept to the same pace as them. Amina was delighted. She couldn't believe it. Here she was travelling along with kangaroos, just as she had wished.

Chapter 2

The kangaroos were completely unconcerned by her presence and continued on their journey. "I must be in the open plains of the Outback," Amina thought, remembering what she had read about Australia.

After some time, the kangaroos stopped by a watering hole. The carpet stopped too. Amina was so close to the animals that she could reach out and touch the furry ears of the kangaroo next to her. Tentatively she stretched out a hand and carefully touched the tip of one ear. The kangaroo looked at her but did not move away, so Amina gently stroked the animal's ears and head. It was a fantastic feeling.

Some of the female kangaroos had babies – or joeys, as they were called – in their pouches. Amina was delighted by the way their little heads poked out from their safe surroundings.

Amina had read quite a few books about Australia and she decided that there were other interesting sights that she wanted to see. "I'd like to visit Uluru now," she said aloud.

Immediately the carpet soared up into the sky and began a new journey.

Uluru was a huge rock that was sacred to the Aboriginals, the native people of Australia. When it came into view, it took Amina's breath away. It was a beautiful reddish pink. She instructed the carpet to take her to see the cave paintings in the rock. The rock art, done by the Aboriginals, was about something that they called 'Dreamtime'. In their folklore this was a time when god-like beings created the land. They believed that magical creatures lived on earth before humans.

The Aboriginals had been great hunters and they travelled throughout the country, using the natural resources with care. They thought that they were part of the land and could not own it. Amina admired the drawings in the cave and then asked the carpet to take her to visit some Aboriginal people.

The group that she met had painted their bodies with vivid patterns. One of the men was making music on a didgeridoo. A didgeridoo is a long, wooden tube that makes a deep droning noise when it is blown into. It was a strange sort of music to Amina's ears, but fascinating nonetheless. Afterwards she looked at some paintings they had done on tree bark. The Aboriginals are famous for these paintings, and they explained to Amina that they stripped the bark off eucalyptus trees and left it to dry before painting the inside. Many of the paintings consisted of coloured dots, mostly in white, yellow and orange. They were very bright and beautiful. Talking about eucalyptus bark made Amina think of koalas and, after she had left the group of Aboriginal people, she asked the carpet to take her to see some of these little furry animals.

The carpet soared up into the air again and after some time entered a forest. Amina knew that koalas ate the leaves of eucalyptus trees. Although these leaves were very poisonous to most animals, their digestive systems were able to deal with the poison. However, eucalyptus leaves aren't very nutritious so, to conserve energy, koalas sleep for up to 16 hours a day. The koalas were doing just that as Amina flew among the trees of the forest. They had thick woolly fur that looked inviting to the touch and Amina thought they smelt of cough drops. Some of them opened a sleepy eye as she hovered on the carpet close by. She was able to stroke several, and marvelled at how soft they felt. She wished that she could take one home with her. It would make a wonderfully cuddly teddy bear.

Amina had read that many of these cute, little animals were killed every year by cars and dogs and she felt sad about that. She knew that they would not be waking up for several hours, so she thought about what else she would like to see. Amina decided that she would like to see some of Australia's famous beaches and then the Great Barrier Reef. The carpet did as she requested and sailed once more up into the air.

Amina looked out over the famous Bondi Beach. She could see hundreds of people enjoying themselves, either relaxing in the sunshine on the sand or surfing in the sea. The sea rolled in again and again as the surfers struggled to stay upright on their boards and ride the waves. It looked like great fun.

The next stop was the Great Barrier Reef, a huge expanse of coral reef that stretched for 1,250 miles. Coral reefs are made up of the hardened skeletons of millions of tiny sea creatures and are home to some of the most beautiful and colourful fish in the sea.

The flying carpet skimmed the surface of the water. There were no people about, and Amina could look down on to the coral and see the amazing fish swimming about. At other times the carpet rose higher and Amina was able to watch the antics of people snorkelling from above. She saw several black- and white-tip reef sharks, and once she thought she saw a great white shark. She was very glad that she was not in the water near that.

Eventually Amina began to feel hungry and thought it was time to head for home.

The journey back seemed to take no longer than a few minutes in spite of the great distance.

Amina was sitting on her bed reading when her mother poked her head round the door. "Your tea is ready," she informed Amina. "You know you really ought to get out and about a bit more. See some sights and enjoy some fresh air," she added.

"Yes, Mum," said Amina, looking very innocent indeed. "I'll try to spend less time shut up in my room."

Chapter 3

The following day, Amina thought long and hard about where she wanted to go on the flying carpet. There were so many interesting and fascinating places in the world that it was difficult to choose, but eventually she decided on China. That was because it was such a vast and varied country, and also she particularly wanted to see a giant panda, while she had the opportunity.

She knew from a book she had read that there were just 700 to 1,000 of these shy animals left in the wild and their natural habitats were gradually being destroyed. They only ate the shoots of the fountain bamboo, which grows in the forests of Sichuan, Yunnan and Tibet, and the forests were being cleared for new building or to grow crops on the land. The Chinese government was trying to help the pandas by creating nature reserves for them and treating them like a national treasure, but Amina was worried that one day there would be none left to see.

Hiding behind the tall bamboo plants, Amina lay quietly on the carpet as she watched the magnificent animals go about their daily business. It was quite difficult to tear herself away from this fascinating sight, but eventually she forced herself to move on.

Amina asked the carpet to make a slight detour in Sichuan province so that she could marvel at the Grand Buddha of Leshan, a giant statue carved into the rock face during the Tang dynasty, around 1,300 years ago. It was believed to have been commissioned by a monk who was concerned about the number of boating accidents in the waters below. This was an area where two rivers met and the waters were very turbulent. The monk thought that the Grand Buddha would watch over the boatmen and keep them safe. The statue had taken 90 years to complete, and Amina wondered how on earth the people living then had managed such an enormous and difficult task without the help of modern machinery. The statue was 71m high and even an ear was 7m long; a big toe was 8.5m.

Amina had a really good view of the statue as the carpet approached it, and she could see people walking around the base. In proportion to the Grand Buddha, they looked like tiny ants. The carpet stopped and Amina got off. She gazed up at the statue, and it did indeed feel as if she was standing next to a giant.

"It's a good job giants don't really exist," she thought to herself. "I know now what it would feel like to meet up with one."

Amina asked the carpet if it would show her some cormorants fishing, and she was soon hovering above a small boat. A man stood upright in the boat, wearing a wide-brimmed hat. Along the edges of the boat four cormorants – large birds – were perched, watching the water intently.

Amina thought that this was an ingenious way to go fishing, much more fun than using a rod or a net. The birds dived into the water and caught fish that they brought back to the boat. They were unable to swallow their catch because of rings tied round their necks, so the fisherman was able to take the fish from them. Amina had read that they were allowed to eat every seventh fish that they caught. She watched the action for a while, then decided it was time to set off for the next destination.

Amina had read about the Terracotta Warriors, and thought that they must be an amazing sight, so a visit to Xi'an was next on her list. This incredible army of a thousand life-size pottery soldiers had been discovered under the ground in 1974, and there may be a further six thousand figures still buried. The army had been created by a wealthy ruler called Shi Huangdi over two thousand years before to protect him in the afterlife, and the soldiers were grouped in battle formation – including some on horseback or in chariots. They carried bronze spears, swords and crossbows. When he became Emperor, Shi Huangdi had ordered 700,000 men to work on his terracotta army and every soldier in the army had a different face. It had been an amazing feat of organisation. Foreigners weren't generally allowed to walk along the rows of the soldiers, so Amina felt very privileged to fly among their ranks, unseen on her flying carpet. It certainly was a fantastic spectacle.

Amina's next stop was in the Forbidden City of Beijing, once home to the Chinese emperors. It was called the Forbidden City because for five hundred years ordinary people were forbidden to enter the palace on pain of death. There are six palaces in the city, with beautiful polished roofs held up by red pillars. Amina flew in through the Wumen Gate. At one time only the emperor could use this gate, and on ceremonial occasions he would be flanked by a guard of elephants. Amina saw the Golden Water stream with its five marble bridges and the fierce-looking lions that guard the Gate of Supreme Harmony. Beyond this gate was a large courtyard where, sometimes, 100,000 people gathered. They had to stand in complete silence while the Emperor sat on his throne. A white marble ramp decorated with dragons led up to the Emperor's magnificent throne room. Amina enjoyed looking at the beautiful treasures and works of art as the carpet transported her around the Forbidden City.

Amina's empty tummy reminded her that it would soon be time for tea, and she had one last sight to see. She wanted to fly alongside the Great Wall of China, at 3,750 miles the longest wall in the world. The wall stands around 7.6m tall and is wide enough for horsemen to ride along it. Riding on the carpet alongside the wall was an exhilarating experience. It seemed to go on and on for ever, but eventually Amina left it behind her as the carpet soared up higher into the sky to take her on the journey back to her home.

Chapter 4

The following day Amina was up bright and early, to the great surprise of her mother. "You're not usually around at this time during half-term," she said to Amina. "What are you planning to do today?"

"Oh, I'd thought I'd go on an African safari," Amina replied.

"In your books," her mother laughed, but that is exactly what Amina planned for her carpet expedition that day. She wanted to see elephants and lions and then the gorillas of the Congo.

"If you're going to be buried in your books all day, I'll probably see you again at tea time," said her mother. "Don't forget to eat something at lunch time."

Amina rushed back to her room as soon as she had finished the last mouthful of cereal. Sitting in the middle of the flying carpet, she gave her instruction, "To the African Savannah, please."

Immediately the carpet soared into the air and out of the window. In no time at all they were above the African Savannah. Amina gazed down on to the grasslands below, looking out for exciting animals. The first one that she saw was a cheetah, the fastest of the big cats. She knew that these swift animals could run at up to 70 miles an hour.

"I'd love to have a race with a cheetah," she told the carpet.

At once the carpet flew close to the cat, startling it. The cheetah set off at top speed with the carpet alongside. Amina shrieked with delight as she and the big cat flew along side by side, "I can't believe that I'm racing with a cheetah," she laughed. The carpet soon veered off in another direction so as not to tire the cheetah too much and instead found a pride of lions for Amina to admire.

The lions were sprawled on the ground, lazing in the warm sunshine. A huge male with a great, shaggy mane opened one eye to glance at the carpet. He gave a yawn, revealing his large, pointed teeth, then closed the eye and went back to sleep. One of the lionesses was cleaning a young cub, gently licking its fur, while a couple of older cubs played together, rolling around on the ground in a furry ball. Amina wished that she could go and play with the cubs – they looked so sweet and cuddly – but she knew this would not be safe and she didn't want to become lunch for the lions.

The carpet moved on, and soon Amina saw a group of giraffes and zebras beneath her. She marvelled at the long legs and necks of the giraffes. They seemed such strange animals in their form and stature. Amina admired the variety of patterns on the zebras' black and white coats. She wished that they were domesticated like horses as she would love to ride on their stripy backs.

Moving on from the giraffes and zebras, the flying carpet took Amina to a herd of elephants, which was being led by an old and large matriarch. Amina marvelled at the length and thickness of her ivory tusks as she led her group to a water hole. Many of the females had young of varying ages and Amina was enraptured by one baby elephant. The little chap wandered in and out of the adults' legs. Every now and then he had to run to keep up with the herd.

When they reached the hole, the elephants wallowed in the water and rolled in the mud, having great fun. They sprayed water from their trunks and the youngsters pushed and splashed one another in enjoyment. One of the youngsters wandered off by herself to do a bit of exploring.

Amina became rather anxious about this lone elephant as she seemed to be straying too far from the protection of the large females. A rustle in the undergrowth close to the young elephant alerted Amina, and she instructed the carpet to take a closer look. Crouched behind a bush and getting ready to attack was a large lion. Amina was desperate. What could she do to save the young elephant?

She told the carpet to dive-bomb the lion. She had seen small birds do this to larger birds of prey and hoped it would work. The carpet zoomed in again and again, down close to the lion's head, then up, turning for a fresh assault. When the carpet was close to the large cat, Amina shouted as loud as she could. The dive-bombing startled the lion, putting him off his attack, and alerted the elephants to the danger. The large adults came stomping along and, seeing the youngster and the big cat close by, rushed at the lion, forcing him to run away.

"Well done, carpet!" Amina said. "We saved the day."

Amina's next stop was to visit a tribe of Maasai. They lived in huts made from poles driven into the ground, then covered in branches and mud and with grass roofs. They were dressed in bright clothes, especially red, and wore beautiful multi-coloured beaded necklaces and bracelets. The Maasai kept herds of sheep and goats and often walked for many miles looking for food and water for their animals.

Amina watched the young Maasai warriors performing their famous jumping dance. Accompanied by the harmonious singing of the rest of the tribe, the young men took turns to leap up and down. Amina was amazed at the heights that they were able to reach, as if they had invisible springs in their feet.

Amina's last visit on her African adventure was to see gorillas in the jungles of the Congo. These gentle giants, with their 1m arm span, fascinated her. She knew that a large male was as strong as four to eight men, but they were very shy and peaceful creatures. Amina watched a mother as she tickled her baby, the youngster squirming in enjoyment. She marvelled at the size and stature of the great silver-back male as he pulled leaves and shoots from the surrounding plants to eat. The gorilla family were making their beds for the night, bending branches to create springy platforms, so Amina bade them farewell and asked the carpet to take her home for tea before her mum returned.

Chapter 5

The following day Amina decided that – having seen the king of the African big cats, the lion – she wanted to see the other king of big cats, the tiger, so she asked the carpet to take her to India.

She was glad, when she did see one, that she was safely on board the carpet and out of harm's way. The animal was huge and majestic. Its muscles rippled beneath its skin as it walked through the jungle and its beautiful striped coat gleamed in the patchy sunlight as it moved through the trees. Amina thought that she had never seen such a magnificent animal in all her life.

Amina asked the carpet to take her to Agra to see the Taj Mahal. This mausoleum was considered by some people to be the most beautiful building in the world. It was built by the emperor Shah Jahan in 1631 in memory of his dead wife, whom he had loved very dearly. The tomb took 22 years to complete and cost around a million pounds.

As the carpet approached the building, Amina gasped in delight. The beautiful white structure with its four columns shone in the bright sunlight. She flew around the Taj Mahal and saw that it was made from white marble in an octagonal shape. Amina admired the intricate mosaics inlaid with precious stones and the cut marble screens, as delicate as lacework.

There was a story that Shah Jahan was determined that no other building would be constructed that could rival the beauty of the Taj Mahal. He had the master craftsmen's hands chopped off after they had completed the mausoleum. Amina did not know if this was true or just a myth.

Amina asked the carpet to take her northwards. She thought that while she was in this part of the world she should see Mount Everest, the tallest mountain in the world.

It was very chilly around the mountain, but the carpet magically generated a heat that kept Amina warm. She watched a group of climbers slowly make their way up one sheer cliff face and was amazed by their skill and the care that they took. Roped together, they moved up the icy, surface centimetre by centimetre. Amina thought that it looked tremendously hard work and she was grateful of the carpet to take her on her ascent to the summit. When she reached there, it truly felt as if she was at the top of the world. The land beneath her looked like a miniature postcard.

Over the remaining days of half-term, Amina travelled to other destinations around the world and saw all kinds of interesting sights. She watched a mother polar bear with two playful cubs at the North Pole and flew alongside a pod of orcas as they swam and leapt through the sea. At the other end of the world, she laughed at the antics of penguins as they waddled along a snowy shore-line and dived into the sea, where they were transformed into sleek, agile swimmers.

Amina flew over the Eiffel Tower in France and the White House in America. She saw smoking volcanoes, tranquil lagoons, stormy seas and majestic mountains. She skimmed over vast, grassy plains and rippling, sandy deserts, and she watched dozens of animals – from slithering snakes to snapping crocodiles, and furry bears to chattering monkeys. For someone interested in other countries, the flying carpet was the best treat in the world.

The end of half-term was looming. Amina dreaded going back to school and not having whole days free to roam the world. However, she comforted herself with the thought that she could make some trips in the evenings when she got home.

She decided to give herself a big treat on the last day of the holiday and instructed the carpet to take her to Disneyland in Florida. When she arrived, she tucked the carpet under her arm and set about enjoying the rides. The magic of the carpet had ensured that she found a pass to all the attractions in her pocket.

There was so much to do and see that Amina didn't know where to start. In the end she began in the Magic Kingdom with the Monsters Inc. Laugh floor. She also tried Space Mountain; the Haunted Mansion, where she was thrilled with all the scary surprises; Big Thunder Mountain Railroad; Jungle Cruise and last, and definitely her favourite, Pirates of the Caribbean. It was a very tired Amina who tumbled into bed that night to dream of all the thrills of Disneyland.

The following day at school seemed endless and Amina was itching to get back to the flying carpet. Arriving home at last, she flung her bag down in the hall and raced up to her bedroom, ready for the next adventure. Opening the door, she saw at once that the carpet was not in its usual place next to her bed. She searched the room, then ran downstairs to the kitchen, where her mother was busily preparing the evening meal.

"Mum, do you know where my carpet is?" Amina asked.

"Why, yes," her mother replied. "The man from the shop came to collect it. Remember, he said you could have it for a week, and then he would need it back for someone else to enjoy."

Amina was devastated. No more exciting trips abroad. Sadly she walked back to her room and flung herself on her bed. As she lay there, she slowly began to feel less sorry for herself. She had enjoyed the best week of her life with the flying carpet and had the most wonderful memories of the places she had visited and the sights she had seen. How many other children could claim such an amazing experience?

With a sigh, Amina rolled off the bed and went downstairs for her meal.

Follow-up work for each chapter

CHAPTER 1

Put the children into groups of 5-6. Tell them to imagine they had a magic carpet and to discuss, in their groups, where they would most like to visit and what they would most like to see there. Call the groups together and ask the children to tell you their destinations to see if there is a favourite place.

CHAPTER 2

Put the children into mixed-ability groups of 4-6. If you are able, read them a story about the Aboriginals' Dreamtime (look up http://australia.pppst.com/dreamtime-stories.html). Ask the children to make up a mythical story, in their groups, about how the world or their country was created. Let the groups in turn relate their stories to the class.

CHAPTER 3

Put the children into groups of 6. Explain that they are going to make up a short, dramatic scene in which they are Chinese fishermen in a boat. They must act or mime travelling along the river in their boat (perhaps they could practise rowing in unison) when they reach turbulent waters and are in danger of sinking. Tell the children they have to convey the fear that they are feeling. They see the Grand Buddha of Leshan and implore him to save them. Does he? They must act out what happens.

CHAPTER 4

Ask the children to choose an animal that they like and write a poem about it. It doesn't have to rhyme. Tell them to think of all the important aspects of their animal (e.g. Is it big, fast, ferocious, graceful?). Encourage them to use interesting descriptive words. They can draw and colour an illustration to go with their poem.

CHAPTER 5

Put the children into mixed-ability groups of 3. Ask them to make up a new ride for Disneyland based, if possible, on a Disney film they have seen. They can make sketches and notes to help explain their rides. They must plan how the attraction looks, what they ride on or in and what happens during the ride.

Ideas for maths

Measuring the Grand Buddha

Put the children into groups of 4-6. Ask them to measure out the Grand Buddha's ear (7m) and his big toe (8.5m) using metre rules or tape measures. How do these compare to their heights? See if the whole class can measure out the Buddha's total height of 71m. Perhaps they could draw him with chalk on the playground.

Around the world

Photocopy the map of the world on template 5.1 (p. 124) for each child. Write the following coordinates on the board and ask the children to find and write down what is at each coordinate on their map of the world:

(C,10) (P,6) (V,2) (H,5) (K,8) (T,11) (D,9) (N,6) (R,8) (G,5) (M,7) (K,12)

(S,10) (F,8) (Q,11) (U,3) (F,7) (L,9) (M,3) (S,4) (J,8) (F,6) (M,11) (R,5)

(P,4) (L,10) (K,7) (M,5) (Q,9) (T,3) (O,10) (M,6) (K,9) (H,3)

Taj Mahal and Chinese pagoda

Photocopy the Taj Mahal in India and the Chinese pagoda on template 5.2 (p. 125) for each child and ask them to complete the missing half.

Two-dice lotto

Put the children into pairs and ask each pair to draw a grid 6 squares by 6 squares. They fill each horizontal line with two-digit numbers using numbers up to six (i.e. first line: 11, 12, 13, 14, 15, 16; second line: 21, 22, 23, 24, 25, 26; third line: 31, 32, 33, 34, 35, 36 and so on up to 66. Using different coloured counters, the children take turns to throw two dice and use the numbers shown in either combination as coordinates. They place a counter on the coordinate unless it is already taken. After a set time or number of throws, they count up their counters to see who has the most on the grid. The pairs can then change round so that there are different players.

Science work

Perfume pots

Give each child a plastic or polystyrene cup. Take them outside and ask them to collect different leaves in their pots. Pour water into the pots and give the children stirrers. Ask them to poke and stir their leaves in the water to create a scent. Do all the pots smell the same?

Hiding Barney

Photocopy the Hiding Barney template, 1.8 (p. 31), on to thin card for each child. Talk to the children about camouflage and why animals might want to blend into their background. Explain that they are going to decorate their card dogs in a way that will make them camouflaged. They may use scraps of material, chalks, paint, crayons or any other medium. They will then take turns to hide their dogs outside for the other children to find. Encourage them to discuss which were the easiest/hardest to locate. It may be a good idea to take the children outside prior to their starting this activity, so that they can look for suitable hiding-places and see the colours that they will need to use.

Other activities

What am I?

Ask the children to wordstorm all the animals they can think of and write the name of each animal on a card. The children take turns to have one of the cards pinned to their back. They turn round to show the card to the rest of the class and then ask questions about their animal until they guess its identity. They might ask, for instance:

> Where do I live?
>
> Am I big or small?
>
> What colour am I?
>
> What do I eat?

What's in your case?

The children work in pairs. Give each pair a Suitcase template, 5.3 (p. 126), photocopied on to A3 paper. They fold the paper in half along the fold line and colour the outside of the case. They then (quietly, so that no one else overhears them) decide what items to write or draw inside their cases that they might take when they go on holiday to another country (e.g. sun cream, sun hat, swimming costume, snorkel). Tell them to use their imagination to think up some unusual items. When they have finished, they join up with another pair and take turns to guess an item in the other pair's suitcase. They get a point for each item correctly guessed.

Maasai warrior

Photocopy the Maasai warrior template, 5.4 (p. 127), for each child to colour.

Flying carpet

Photocopy the Flying carpet, template 5.5 (p. 128), for each child.

Around the world word search

Give each child a copy of the Around the world word search template 5.6 (p. 129). Instructions are given on the sheet.

Active games

Get to the point

You will need plenty of space for this game. Number cards 1–6 and place them around the room or playground. The children stand with you in the centre. Tell them to move in one particular way (jumping, skipping, crawling, walking backwards, hopping, walking sideways, walking heel to toe or on tiptoes). Roll a large floor dice. The children have to move in the manner designated to the number shown. The last to arrive is out and rolls the dice next time. The children stay where they are until you tell them the next way to move and roll the dice again.

Guess that animal

Ask the children to call out different animals. Write each one on a slip of paper, so that you have at least one for each child in the group. Fold the slips in half and place them in a container. Ask the children to volunteer, one at a time, to take a slip out of the container and mime the animal shown for the others to guess. If they cannot guess, they can ask questions to help them.

Bug-catcher

Count the number of children in the class. You need a number divisible by 6; if there are more, the remainder are bug-catchers (e.g. with 27 children, 3 are designated as bug-catchers) who stand in the centre of the playing area. Explain to the rest of the children that they are to move around the bug-catchers. When you shout "Bugs together 1, 2, 3", they must get into groups of 6, standing in rows of 2, one behind the other, to represent the legs of an insect (i.e. three sets of pairs). The bug-catchers must remain still until after you have called the number 3 (you may vary how quickly you call the numbers to allow more or less time for the bugs to get together). They then run around the space and tag any unattached legs. Those either sit out or help the bug-catchers. Continue until you have only one complete bug left, which is the winning one.

Slippery snakes

Divide the class into three or four equal teams. Team members stand one behind the other, grasping the waist of the child in front to form snakes. The object of the game is for each snake to try to grow longer by gobbling up the tail of another snake. To do that the child at the front of the snake must put their hands on the waist of the child at the back of another snake. When that happens, the child that is gobbled up must let go and become the new head of the capturing snake. The snakes twist and turn to try and preserve their own tails while capturing the tails of others. When there is one snake left, or the children are exhausted, count the number of children in each snake to se which is the longest.

Match the country

Make up sets of small cards that can be attached to the children's backs. Each set has items that relate to a particular country. The following sets are for a class of 30 children:

1   Chinese warrior, Great Wall of China, chopsticks, giant panda, Grand Buddha of Leshan

2   kangaroo, koala, boomerang, didgeridoo, Aboriginal

3   tiger, Taj Mahal, Mount Everest, Indian curry, Emperor Shah Jahan

4   lion, elephant, Maasai warrior, gorilla, giraffe.

5   Eiffel Tower, frog's legs, French wine, garlic, Paris

6   Disneyland, Pirates of the Caribbean, Mickey Mouse, Space Mountain, Big Thunder Mountain Railroad.

The children stand in a long line. Pin a card to the back of each child. Explain that they are to form groups of 5, each with related cards. On your command they have to organise themselves into the six sets of different countries. Depending on age and ability, you can leave them to work out the countries without any help, you can tell them the names of the six countries, or you can list the sets for each country on the board.

Art

Aboriginal dot art

Enlarge the Aboriginal crocodile template, 5.7 (p. 130), and draw round it on to black paper for each child. The children colour in the body in a dot pattern, using either lengths of dowel or a finger and yellow, white and orange paint only. If possible, print an example of aboriginal art from a computer to show them an example.

Chinese dragon

Each child makes a Chinese dragon, using a copy of template 5.8 (p. 131). Display the completed dragons on a suitable background.

Chinese clay warrior head

The children make clay warrior heads. They start by forming a ball of scrunched-up newspaper, stuck together with sticky tape. They cover the ball with a rolled-out layer of clay and add the features of a face. Remind them to give their Chinese warrior a top-knot.

Lion

Photocopy the Lion template, 5.9 (p. 132), on to card for each child. The children cut out and colour in the lion and then cut and attach lengths of brown, yellow and orange wool to create a mane. Finally the head of the lion is bent forward and the mane slotted over the neck.

Around the world map

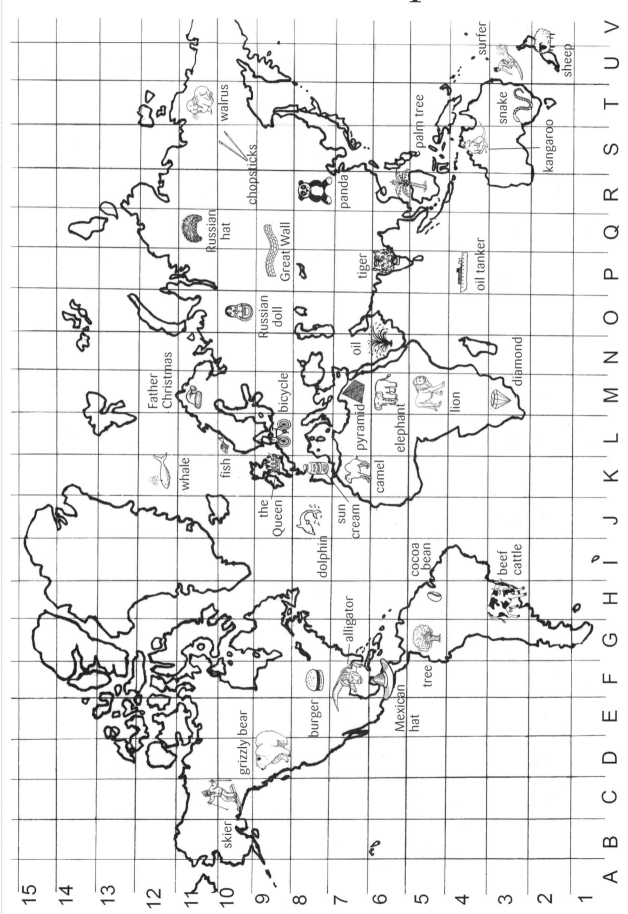

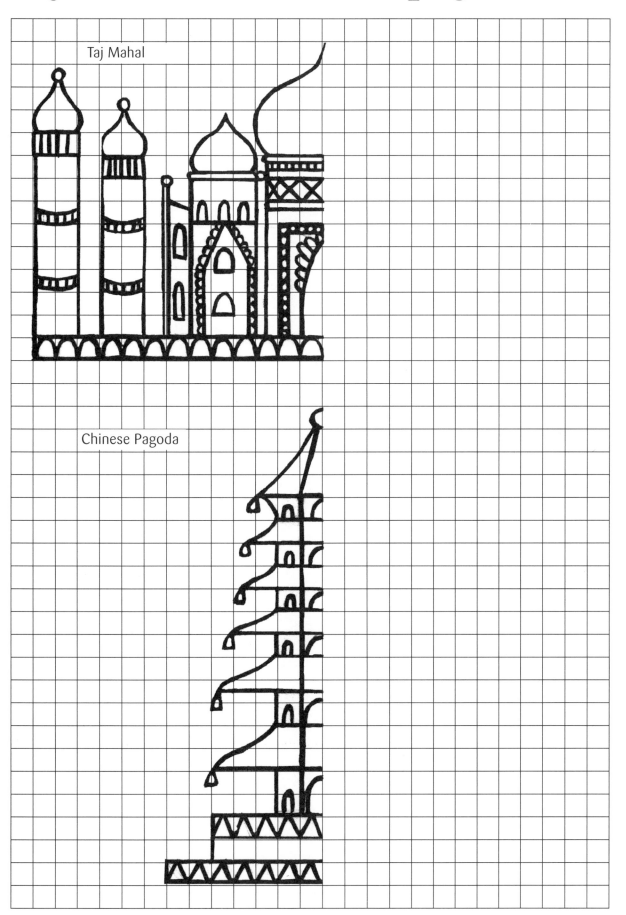

Amina and the flying carpet   125

Taj Mahal and Chinese pagoda

Taj Mahal

Chinese Pagoda

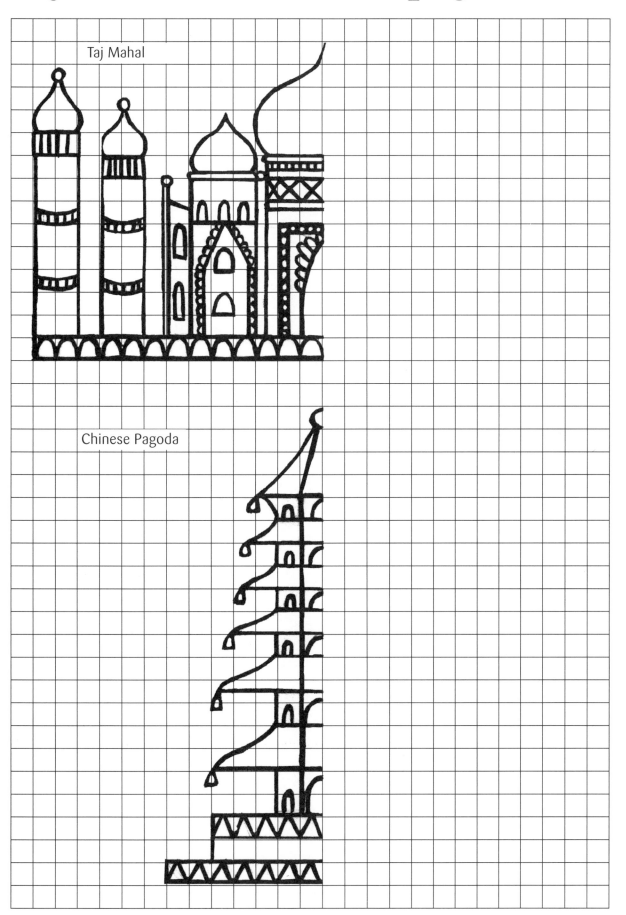

© *End-of-Term Projects*   LDA

Suitcase

Draw the items you would pack for your holiday inside the suitcase.

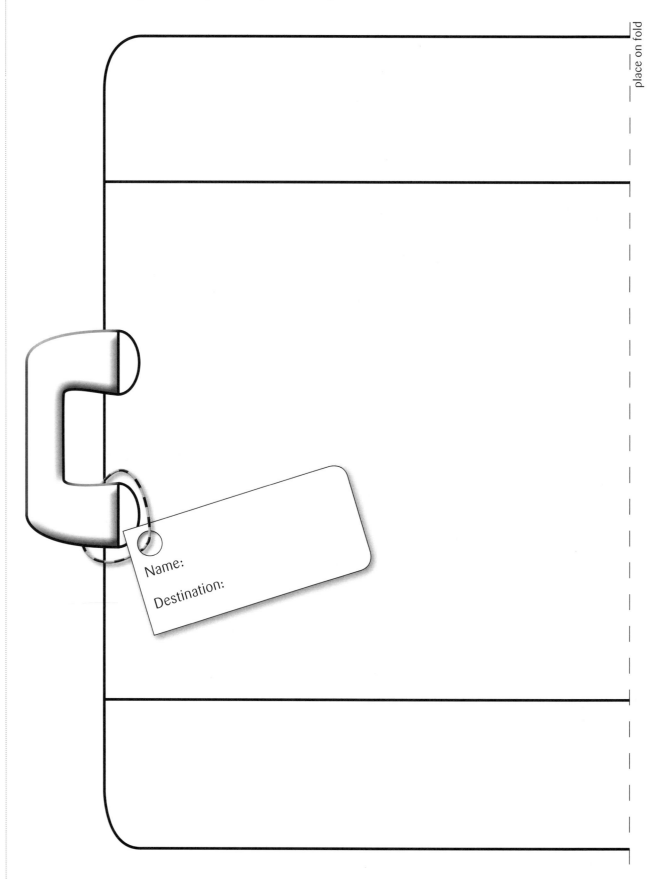

place on fold

Name:

Destination:

Maasai warrior

Colour the warrior using bright colours.

5.5

Flying carpet

Draw a pattern or picture on the flying carpet and colour it.

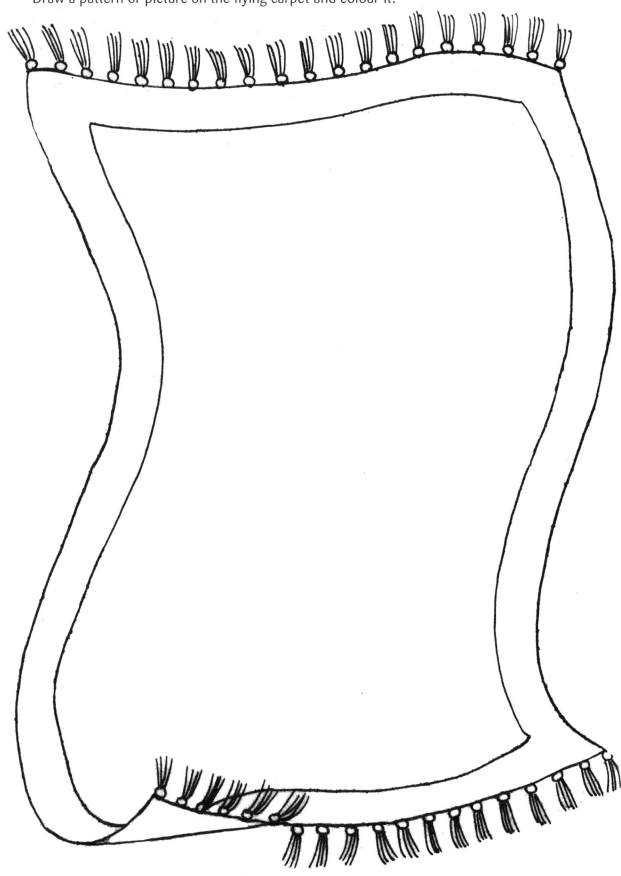

Around the world word search

T	A	B	O	R	I	G	I	N	A	L	E
P	R	U	W	J	I	W	O	N	S	N	J
L	A	D	L	P	O	K	E	O	N	A	S
R	D	D	I	N	G	O	W	O	P	K	N
T	O	H	E	O	I	A	I	A	S	E	A
U	G	A	X	R	W	L	N	P	U	D	K
B	A	U	S	T	R	A	L	I	A	R	E
L	P	Y	O	H	X	S	P	N	M	L	R
J	G	L	O	P	D	Q	A	U	R	S	E
M	R	F	L	O	W	C	H	I	N	A	G
J	U	N	G	L	E	R	D	E	L	H	I
P	B	O	I	E	L	E	P	H	A	N	T

AUSTRALIA   KOALA   CANADA   RIO   WOLF   PAGODA   TIGER
NORTH POLE   ELEPHANT   LION   ABORIGINAL   BUDDHA   DINGO
CHINA   OWL   SNAKE   PIG   JAPAN   IGLOO   GODS   DELHI
JUNGLE   SNOW   GRUB   FLY

Words read horizontally from left to right, vertically and diagonally up or down.
Some of the letters are used in more than one word.

5.7

Aboriginal crocodile

Chinese dragon puppet

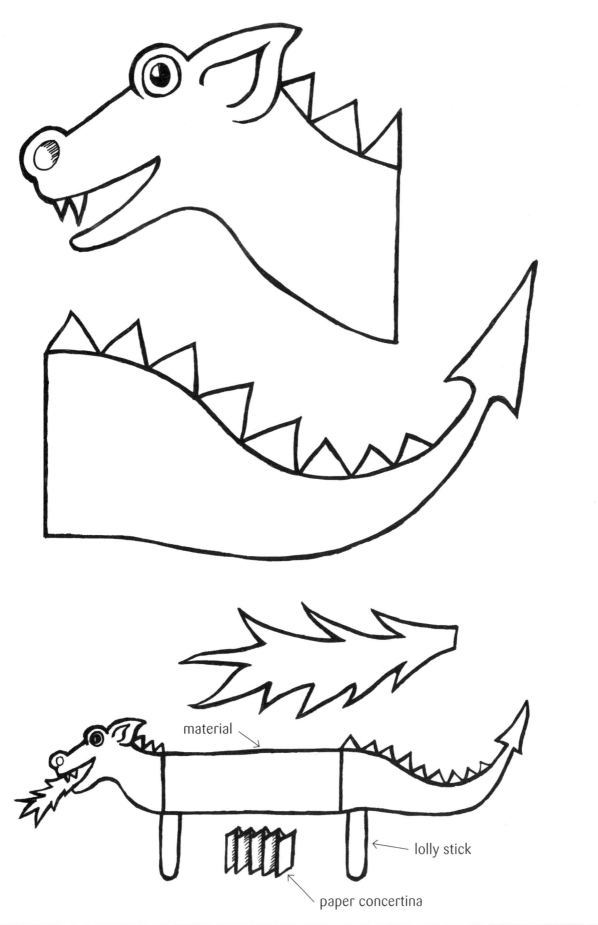

material

lolly stick

paper concertina

5.9

Lion

cut

place on fold of card

mane

Juan and Captain Bartholomew Roberts

A tale of piracy on the high seas

Chapter 1

My name is Juan, and I was 10 years old when my story began. I lived with my sister Rosa, having lost both my parents. My father, a fisherman, was killed in an accident at sea and my mother died in a cholera epidemic. My sister, who was just 15, worked hard to provide for us. She was very talented with a needle and her fine stitching was greatly in demand with local people. Our neighbours – good, kind folk – did what they could to help us and often gave us food, but we were not a rich community and money was scarce.

I would have liked to join a fishing crew to make my own contribution to our household, but my sister would not hear of it. "I've lost my father to the cruel seas," she said to me. "I will not lose my only brother as well. Besides, you are much too young to go out on the rough sea."

I didn't think I was too young. Other boys of my age went out with their fathers or uncles, but it was true that I was very small and slight in stature for my age. I had long-lashed, green eyes and curly light brown hair. The older women clucked over me, saying that I looked like an angel. I hated my appearance. I wanted to be strong and tough and capable of hard work.

Sometimes I walked down to the beach to watch the fisherman set off in their small boats, and I was filled with envy. Their vessels skimmed over the undulating waves that were glinting in the sunlight. They talked and laughed among themselves as they went about their business and returned later in the day with their catch of silver fish. I would be so proud to bring home a few of the fish for Rosa to clean and cook for our supper.

She would not allow me on the sea, so I could only sigh and watch them go.

At times larger ships anchored off our coast and sometimes these belonged to pirates. The people in our small town were much afraid of these marauding bandits as there were many gruesome tales of their cruelty and wickedness. Occasionally a party of pirates rowed ashore to restock their food supplies. The local people scurried around to find whatever they required and see them off as quickly as possible. My neighbours were always most obliging to these unwelcome visitors. They did not want to upset them for fear of terrible reprisals.

My story began in 1720. The day was warm and sunny when I rose one day. Rosa told me that the townsfolk were rushing around in a panic, hiding their valuables and their choicest cuts of meat. A pirate ship had been sighted off our coastline and everyone was worried in case the crew came ashore for provisions.

Having breakfasted, I strolled down to the small harbour to watch the comings and goings there. I sat atop a pile of ropes on the quayside that made a comfortable chair for me. The fishermen had already left when I saw an unfamiliar boat approaching with eight men aboard, rowing hard together. From their clothing I could tell they were crew from the pirate vessel. With a quaking heart, I slid from my seat and hid behind some barrels standing close by. Accompanied by much laughing and shouting, the pirates came ashore and tied up their boat, making their way then along the path towards the houses.

I returned to my vantage point, ready to hide once again when I heard the pirates returning from their shopping trip. The day was very warm and little was happening around me to capture my attention. I must have dozed off because I was suddenly awakened by loud shouts, and then I felt rough hands.

Two of the pirates had grabbed me by my arms and legs and dragged me from my seat of coiled ropes. The more I squirmed and shouted, the harder they held me. One of the other pirates removed the kerchief from his head and tied it around my mouth as a gag. "We don't want him alerting the whole neighbourhood, do we?" he chuckled.

After carrying me down to the quayside, the pirates threw me into the bottom of their boat, then climbed in beside me. I tried to wriggle through their legs and dive out of the boat, but there too many of them and they were too strong. Soon several placed their feet on me to keep me still as they rowed with their strong arms back to their ship.

I could imagine the shoreline receding, and I thought in sorrow of my poor sister Rosa. What would she think had happened to me? Would she guess that the visiting pirates had taken me? My thoughts then turned to my own fate. What did the pirates want with me? Would I be beaten or forced to walk the plank? Would I die of a horrible disease alone at sea with no one there that I loved to care for me?

I glanced up at the burly men in the boat. They looked a villainous bunch of tough cut-throats. One of the pirates saw me looking at him, and surprised me by giving me a huge, gap-toothed grin. "Don't worry, me lad," he said to me. "We ain't goin' to slit you open and feed your gizzard to the fish. You'll be all right with us."

By this time we had reached the side of the pirate ship. A rope ladder hung down over the side. One of the pirates threw me over his shoulder, as if I were no more than an empty suit of clothes, and began to climb up. As he made his way higher, I was able to glimpse the distant shoreline of my home and see for the last time the familiar buildings and features of the landscape. Climbing over the side, the pirate deposited me, none too gently, on the deck.

Thus was I kidnapped by a band of pirates.

Chapter 2

I looked up to a sea of faces as all the crew members crowded round to see what their ship-mates had brought back from their visit to shore.

"What's this?" one pirate shouted. "Have you brought us back a wee girlie this time?"

I blushed red with embarrassment. How I hated my appearance!

"This young fellow will make a fine replacement for Charlie," said one of my captors. "Cap'n'll be delighted, I reckon."

He pushed me forwards towards one of the men surrounding me, who looked rather cleaner and better dressed than most of the crew members.

"Here, Henry," he said, "p'raps you'd like to do the introductions." He burst into loud guffaws of laughter.

Henry took my arm. "Come with me, lad," he said to me in a kindly voice. He led me below deck and knocked on the door of a cabin.

"Enter," commanded a voice from inside.

Opening the door, Henry pushed me in, then followed behind. "New tea-boy for you, Captain," he announced. "Crew brought him back with them just now."

Seated behind a mahogany desk was the Captain. He was dark, and as he stood up I could see that he was tallish in stature. He came around the desk to have a closer look at me, putting his hand under my chin to tilt my face upwards towards his. "Can you make good tea and move quietly?" he asked me.

"I should think so, sir," I responded. I was quaking in my shoes.

"Then you've nothing to be afeared of," he told me. He stood upright and grinned. "Captain Bartholomew Roberts, at your service. What are you called?" he went on, offering me his hand.

I took his hand tentatively and he gave mine a vigorous shake. "Juan, sir," I told him.

"Henry will show you your duties. Off you go now, Juan," he said.

I left the cabin with Henry. I could scarce believe what was happening. This morning I had awoken in my own bed and breakfasted with my sister as usual. Now, but a few hours later, I was aboard a pirate ship and destined for a very different life.

As he instructed me in my duties, Henry told me a little about the Captain. "He's not a bad sort," he said, "as long as you work hard and are loyal to him. There's some captains out there would shoot you dead if the weather was bad or they had a headache from too much rum. Captain Roberts prefers tea to rum. He knows that rum muddles your thinking and you need your wits about you to run a successful pirate ship. He was captured himself, you know. He was an ordinary seaman and was taken by Captain Davis but a year ago. Ordinary sailors have a terrible time. The Navy pays very little and conditions are harsh and poor. Many of them opt to become pirates because the rewards are greater." Henry chuckled at this.

"Anyway, both he and Captain Davis are Welsh and they often used to talk in their native tongue. He was a very good navigator and soon he became the Captain's right hand man. When Captain Davis was killed in an ambush some months later, the crew elected Bartholomew Roberts to be their new boss."

Over the next few days I learnt the duties I was to perform for the Captain. Compared to the hard work of most of the crew, my own workload was very light. Most importantly, I had to be available to make tea as Captain Roberts drank prodigious amounts of this beverage. I also kept his cabin clean and tidy. I was given a bolster and blanket and I slept on the floor outside his cabin, which was better than the cramped, smelly quarters shared by the other pirates.

It took me a while to get used to the food on board. The pirates' diet at sea consisted mainly of tuna, dolphin and turtle. When they put into port, they took on fresh fruit like pineapples and papayas and any vegetables that were available, and they replenished their own stores from captured ships. They also ate hard tack – a horrible, tough biscuit that they sometimes softened by boiling with rum and brown sugar to make a porridge. A favourite dish was salamagundi, a meal of fish, meat and turtle with herbs, oil and spiced wine. They served this with pickled onions, cabbage, grapes and olives. I grew to like it very much.

Most of the crew wore calf-length, loose trousers and plain or checked blue and white shirts. In cold weather they added short jackets of heavy, blue cloth. The men wore woollen caps or kerchiefs on their heads and many favoured gold earrings. They had many stories to account for wearing such jewellery. They said the gold would pay for their funeral if they were killed, and piercing a particular point on their ear helped with sea-sickness or improved their eye-sight, but I think it was just the fashion. On board ship the men were barefooted, this being safer for climbing the rigging or walking on wet decks than the slippery soles of shoes. They might wear canvas or leather shoes when going ashore to spend their ill-gotten gains.

By and large the pirates were kind to me. Perhaps the circumstance of having a young lad on board softened their normally hard hearts. Maybe they thought of their own children many hundreds of miles away and felt sorry for me.

A short time after I joined the crew, a Portuguese ship was sighted and the men prepared for action. I was to witness my first battle and I was filled with great fear and trepidation.

Chapter 3

The Captain dressed in his finest clothes in preparation for the battle to come. I learnt later that this was a tradition with him. He liked to face the enemy "dressed to kill".

He wore a fitted long coat and knee breeches, a fine waistcoat of crimson damask and a tricorn hat with a red feather. On his feet were a highly polished pair of buckled shoes. To complete the ensemble he added gold chains, a sword and two pistols. He certainly presented a fine figure of a man.

He instructed me to stay below decks (as if in my fear I needed this command) saying, "I do not want to lose my tea-boy so soon, Juan."

The crew members readied the guns and stood by their stations. As our ship approached the Portuguese sloop, a pirate unfurled the Jolly Roger, a sight to strike fear into the heart of any able seaman. By and large, pirate ships were greatly feared because they generally carried more men and bigger guns than other vessels.

The noise of the ensuing battle was terrifying to me, even below decks. The cannon boomed and there was much shouting and clashing of steel against steel. The pirates were victorious and captured a chest of gold moidores and a gold cross set with diamonds that had been destined for the King of Portugal. Captain Roberts added the cross to his accessories.

The crew transferred to the captured sloop after this and, buoyed up by his recent successes, the Captain named her *The Fortune*. His good fortune almost ended very quickly thereafter, though, when his vessel and another pirate ship, *The Sea King*, were engaged in battle by two well-armed vessels out of Barbados. The people of that island had had enough of the piracy in their waters, and the inhabitants had raised money to equip two ships to fight the pirates.

On seeing the fire power of the Barbadian vessels, the *Sea King* made a swift escape, leaving *The Fortune* to be set on by both ships. A mighty battle followed. It had me cowering under the Captain's bed, and both our ship and our crew were badly mauled. We were lucky to escape at all. When it ended *The Fortune* limped to Dominica to be repaired. Twenty of our men died that day and Captain Roberts was most saddened by the loss.

He ordered a new flag to be made that depicted him standing atop a skull under which were the initials *ABH*. These, I learned, stood for "A Barbadian Head" and his promise to take revenge on the islanders one day in the future.

Leaving Dominica, the Captain decided to take the ship north, to Newfoundland, out of harm's way. There followed a period of magnificent success for the pirates and they captured many vessels. They transferred to one of the captured ships that had 16 guns, then a month later they took 9 or 10 French vessels and relocated again, to a ship with 26 cannon. Such was their confidence that they renamed this ship *The Good Fortune* and, as their success continued, two months later it became *The Royal Fortune*.

By now the infamy of Captain Bartholomew Roberts was well known and he was considered the most successful pirate to sail the seas. He was known by the nick-name of Black Bart, but he was not an evil man like the pirate Edward Teach, who was known as Blackbeard, and whose reputation for cruelty was feared on both land and sea.

The pirates enjoyed their share of the captured booty and spent time ashore carousing and wasting their ill-gotten gains. They drank and gambled and many lost the treasures that they had won, but the Captain did not join in their merry-making. He was too sensible for that.

The crew enjoyed many types of drink such as bumboo, a mixture of rum, water, sugar and nutmeg. Another favourite was rumfustian, a blend of raw eggs with gin, sherry, sugar and beer. I did have a taste of these concoctions when offered, but I must confess that they were not to my liking. I do not think I have the constitution to be a good (or perhaps I should say bad) pirate.

So, all was well aboard *The Royal Fortune*. The pirates relaxed on board, between skirmishes, by listening to music, playing cards and rolling the dice. The musicians were greatly in demand on board and would play their flutes, drums and fiddles for many hours for the crew's enjoyment, although Captain Roberts had granted them a rest day each week in which to recover.

The crewmen were great dancers, and performed the most vigorous jigs, their feet flying across the decks, almost faster than the eye could follow. Some of the dances had many complicated steps, twists and turns, but I was able to learn a few simple moves under the pirates' tutelage. They always urged me to have a go and clapped my efforts, although I think they were being kind to me rather than giving applause because my dancing was worthy of it.

If the crew were feeling bored, they liked nothing better than to hold mock trials with the pirates playing the roles of judge and jury. I think that on occasion, they entered into the spirit of the trials so thoroughly that the accused became truly afeared for his life.

The days melted one into the other and I gradually grew accustomed to my life on board. I never got used to the sound of the battles raging around me, though, and each time we engaged with other crews I was terrified in case our ship was sunk and I was plunged into the sea and a watery death.

I thought often of my dear sister Rosa and wished I was back safe and sound in my own home again.

Chapter 4

During the calm times, between our sea battles, the crew had to maintain the ship. There was always work to be done to keep *The Royal Fortune* ship-shape. Sails had to be patched when they were torn in battle or damaged by storms, and ropes had to be spliced – that is, joined together into one length by interweaving strands. Keeping the ship watertight was the most important job for the crew members – no one wanted us to take in water and sink. They made sure that the seams were regularly treated by hacking out the old oakum (the unpicked fibres from rope) and replacing it with new oakum which they drove into the seams with a caulking iron. The seam was then sealed tight with hot pitch.

Sometimes we sailed into a harbour, where the ships could be careened (turned over). Repairs could be more easily carried out then and the hull could be scraped to remove the barnacles that clung to its surface and slowed the ship down, and the worms that made tiny holes.

My duties remained light. I maintained Captain Roberts' cabin and prepared his tea, so I cannot complain that I was overworked.

This was a time of plenty for the crew and they were happy and full of jokes and laughter. There was an abundance of good food to go round and a full stomach always makes for a contented man. Henry told me that it was not always the case – sometimes food was in very short supply. He told me of a famous story about the pirate captain Sir Henry Morgan's crew in 1670. They had run out of provisions and were in danger of starving. In the end they cut up their leather satchels, soaked the strips, then tenderised them by beating and rubbing the leather with stones. They scraped off the hair and roasted or grilled the strips before cutting them into bite-sized pieces. Not very appetising – but it saved them from starvation.

During September and October of 1721 we captured 15 French and English ships and Captain Roberts' reputation continued to rise.

Some of the crew of the captured vessels joined our pirate crew and the ranks were swelled quite considerably. It was a motley crew of men aboard *The Royal Fortune* by now. They were of all colours and from many different countries, but it is a strange thing that a common lingo seemed to prevail, being a mixture of seamen's words and a hotchpotch of other languages. At any rate, everybody seemed to understand everyone else well enough to perform their duties and rub along amicably.

By June 1721 we were sailing off the coast of Africa. In spite of the fact that, as pirates, we were outlaws, there were many towns that were more than happy to welcome us into their ports and relieve us of our gold.

One memorable incident happened during this time, when we were chased by two French ships, one of 10 guns and the other a 16 gunner. Such was the skilled seamanship of Captain Roberts that, not only did he avoid capture by the French, but he was able to turn the tables and capture both of their ships. He also captured two more big ships and commandeered one of the frigates as the next, new *Royal Fortune*.

During November and December of 1721, the crew careened *The Royal Fortune* and spent two months resting and relaxing. Word had come to Captain Roberts that the Royal Navy had sent two well-armed ships to the area, specifically to capture him. HMS *Swallow* and HMS *Weymouth* were armed to the teeth. In fact HMS *Swallow* had 60 guns and a crew of specially chosen, brave fighting men. The Navy were determined to stop Black Bart once and for all.

In January 1722 we pirates were on the prowl again, looking for new ships to capture, and on 9 February we were rewarded with a vessel called *The Neptune*.

Generally speaking, my master was not cruel to the people on board the many ships he took and, in fact, he rarely commandeered their vessels. He removed the booty and let them go, and if he did decide to keep their ships, then he traded one of his in exchange. That particular night he dined with Captain Hill of *The Neptune* while his crew celebrated by downing gallons of rum and becoming much the worse for wear.

The following day, 10 February, I was serving tea to Captain Roberts and Captain Hill when a pirate knocked on his door to announce the sighting of HMS *Swallow* coming in their direction. The Captain knew that we were greatly outgunned and could not engage in fire with the man o' war. Our only hope was to slip past the heavily armed ship and escape.

Being Captain Bartholomew Roberts, brave and fearless, he did not leap to his feet in a panic, but took the customary time to don all his finery.

"How do I look, Juan?" he asked me before stepping out on deck.

"You look magnificent, as usual," I replied.

The plan was to manoeuvre past the *Swallow*, allowing her just one chance at our broadsides before making for the open seas. However, the poor state of the crew following their night of heavy drinking resulted in a mistake by the helmsman that allowed the *Swallow* a second opportunity to fire. I heard the boom of the guns and then a shout from the deck.

"The Captain's down," yelled the voice. "Captain Roberts is hit."

I held my breath in fear and panic. If we were taken by the Navy, what would happen to me? Would I be hanged as a pirate and therefore a villainous criminal?

Chapter 5

I could no longer remain in my hiding-place; I had to find out what was happening. I slipped out on deck. Everywhere was chaos. The noise of firing cannon, the smell of gunpowder, dense choking smoke and the loud shouting of all the pirates were overwhelming. I scanned the deck, searching the confusion of bodies for any sighting of Captain Roberts. Then I caught a glimpse of a red feather. The Captain's hat lay on the ground. Close by the hat I saw helmsman Stephenson. He was instructing two other crew members to help him lift a body. With a gasp of dismay, I recognised the red waistcoat of the Captain.

The three men hoisted the body aloft, and with a swing of their arms tossed it overboard. I watched as my master was cast into the frothing, churning sea.

Helmsman Stephenson turned and saw me as I cowered against the main mast. He hurried over. "Come on, lad," he said gently. "This is no place for a child."

He led me gently back to the cabin. I was in tears by now and cried to him, "Why did you throw Captain Roberts so cruelly into the sea?"

"'Twas not cruel. 'Twas the Cap'n's wish. He allus said as how he didn't want his body to fall into enemy hands. When his end came he wanted to be buried at sea. 'Tis what he woud've wished."

So saying he left me once more in the cabin and returned to the fray. The battle raged above me for a good two hours. The boom of the cannon and loud shouts of the men were terrifying to listen to. Finally I heard a massive crack and thud. The main mast had been felled and I knew the end was near.

The pirates surrendered to HMS *Swallow*. Their Captain, Chaloner Ogle was not well pleased that Captain Roberts had been thrown overboard – he had wanted to see the pirate in person. However, a search of the seas failed to reveal any sign of the body.

The pirates were rounded up. Amazingly, only three, including our Captain, had been killed in the fierce battle. That left 272 men who would face trial for their crimes.

The world was stunned, pirates and ordinary folks alike, by the death of Black Bart. Everyone had thought him invincible. During his three years of piracy on the high seas, he had captured over four hundred ships and £50,000,000 of loot. He was considered by many to be the most successful pirate captain of all time.

I need not have feared for my life. When the authorities heard my story of how I had been snatched from my home, and in consideration of my tender age, I was acquitted of all crimes. Over a third of the captured men were also acquitted as they too had been forced, against their wills, to join forces with the pirate crew. Of the remainder some were sent to prison for a time and the others, those considered to be truly villainous pirates, were hanged.

Captain Chaloner Ogle of HMS *Swallow* was knighted for his role in defeating Bartholomew Roberts as the British government was glad to restore safety on the seas for their merchant ships.

As for my own part, I felt a mixture of relief and sadness. I was glad that my pirating days were at an end as I did not care for robbing other people, but I had grown to be quite fond of my Captain and was sad that he had died – although I am sure that he would have preferred his pirate's end and a watery grave to the hangman's noose. Even though he was a thief and a plunderer, Bartholomew Roberts was considered by most to be a gentleman, fair and just. He was more considerate to both his own men and those he captured than any other pirate captain and, above all, he was a brilliant and quick-thinking seaman. His death marked the end of the golden age of piracy.

The authorities made arrangements for me to return on an outgoing ship to my homeland. I was excited at the thought of seeing my dear sister Rosa and all my friends and neighbours again. Day after day I scanned the horizon for a glimpse of the familiar landmarks that would welcome me back, and my impatience was great.

At last, though, we arrived at our destination. I scrambled down the gang-plank and ran all the way to our small cottage. Bursting through the door, I surprised Rosa, who was putting a tray of rolls into the oven. She dropped the tray with a loud clang, and the mounds of dough scattered across the floor. Her eyes grew wide with disbelief.

"Juan! Is that really you?" she gasped.

We flew into each other's arms and hugged and laughed until we were exhausted. "I never thought to see you again, Juan," she told me. "I was so miserable thinking of you on board a pirate ship."

Over the next few days I settled back into my life at home and told Rosa and my neighbours all about my adventures with Captain Bartholomew Roberts.

That should have been the end of my story, but it wasn't, not quite. Some time later a tale began to circulate concerning Black Bart. 'Twas said that he had not in fact died on *The Royal Fortune*. Instead, the body of another pirate was dressed in his clothes and thrown overboard by helmsman Stephenson, who was in on the plot. Captain Roberts, meanwhile, dressed in ordinary seaman's clothes, was rowed to *The Neptune* by its skipper, Captain Hill. He is said to have paid the governor of the region a gold cross studded with diamonds to effect his escape.

Some time later, Captain Hill turned up in Barbados with an anonymous passenger and paid the governor there 50 ounces of gold dust for a safe passage to Florida. I do not know if this story was true. I hoped that it was, and that Captain Bartholomew Roberts was living a comfortable life somewhere, his pirate past a secret left behind him.

Follow-up work for each chapter

Chapter 1

Put the children into groups of 5–6. Tell them to imagine that they are villagers who live by the sea. One day they see a pirate ship anchored off the coast and pirates approaching their village in a rowing boat. Ask the children to work out a plan of action. What would they do? How would they respond to the pirates? Call the groups together and let each, in turn, describe their plan.

Chapter 2

Tell the children each to imagine that they are a pirate captain. Ask them to think of a suitable pirate nick-name and describe what they would wear. They can draw a picture and either label the clothes or write an accompanying description.

Chapter 3

Put the children into groups of around 6. Explain to them that they are going to make up a short drama about being on board a pirate ship. They should elect one child as the captain (this is how they did it on real pirate ships). The rest are crew members.

Tell the groups to think of a situation to enact (e.g. chasing and capturing another ship, evading capture by a man o' war, weathering a storm at sea). When the children have practised their scenes, they can show them to the rest of the class.

Chapter 4

Put the children into pairs. Tell them that together they are to imagine that they are a pirate. They should write two lists of the things that they (1) do and (2) do not like about a pirate's life. At the end of the session, let the children share their lists with the rest of the class. Is there a clear favourite feature of a pirate's life and a least liked feature?

Chapter 5

Give each child the story sheet template, 6.1 (p. 149), photocopied on to A3 paper, to complete.

Ideas for maths work

Pirate's necklace

Put the children into small groups or pairs for this activity. They will need beads, laces to thread the beads on and a stop-watch. (Try borrowing beads and laces from the Reception class.) The children take turns to see how many beads they can thread on to the lace in a given time (1–3 minutes, depending on age). They then measure the length of their necklace to see who has made the longest. You could have a class competition, to see who is the champion necklace-maker.

Continue the pattern

Photocopy the Continue the pattern template, 6.2 (p. 150), for each child. They continue the pattern on each line and make up one of their own for the blank line. They can colour the sheets when they have finished their patterns.

Pirate sums

Photocopy the Pirate sums template, 6.3 (p. 151), for each child. The sums 1–5 are graded a), b) and c) for level of difficulty. Children may choose which letter they answer (explain that in each question they must answer two parts with the same letter), or they may do all three if they wish. Questions 6 and 7 are intended as an extension; children can do either or both of these, depending on age and level of attainment.

Times the dice

The children play this activity in pairs. Try to pair children with the same level of attainment in maths. They need a 100 square, a dice, a stop-watch and different-coloured counters or pens. They take turns to throw the dice. For the numbers 2–6 they have a set time to put their counters on the 100 square or mark with a pen numbers that are in the relevant times table. You can determine the time from 10 to 30 seconds according to their levels of attainment. If the number 1 is turned up, they miss a go. At the end of the allotted time, they count up their counters or marks to see who is the winner. They can swap pairs and play with different children at the same attainment level.

Treasure Island

Give each child a copy of the Treasure Island template, 6.4 (p. 152), and ask them to draw on it at the correct coordinates the features listed. They may write down a set of coordinates on a separate piece of paper to mark where their treasure is buried and ask their class-mates to each have a turn to guess the spot.

Science work

Making a compass

The children should work in pairs. They will need a clear plastic cup, a pencil, a bar magnet and a needle and thread. They need to stroke one end of the magnet along the needle 30 to 40 times in the same direction. They tie one end of the thread to the centre of the needle and the other end to the centre of the pencil. The pencil is then balanced on the rim of the cup to allow the needle to hang freely. The thickest end of the needle will point in a northerly direction.

Ask the children to check if all their needles are facing the same way.

Take the children to stand in the middle of the playground. Ask them to write down some of the buildings and other features around them, and then to decide which direction each feature is from where they are standing.

Salty sea

Put the children into small groups. Each group needs a large beaker containing the same measured amount of water, an egg and salt. The activity is to demonstrate what makes the sea more buoyant than fresh water. Ask the children to place the egg gently into the water. It will sink. Ask them to add spoonfuls of salt to the water until the egg floats. How many spoonfuls of salt were needed?

Other activities

Treasure chest

Photocopy the Treasure chest template, 6.5 (p. 153), for each child. Ask them to draw in it the possessions that they most treasure. With older children you could ask them to think of more abstract concepts such as good health, kindness and sharing, and either to write or to draw representative items and label them.

Pirate board game

Put the children into pairs or small groups of 3-4. Photocopy the Pirate board game template, 6.6 (p. 154), on to A3 paper for each pair or small group. They can colour the sheet first, then play the game. They will each need a different-coloured counter, and each group needs a dice.

Spot the difference

Photocopy template 6.7 (p. 155) for each child. Tell them there are 16 differences between the pictures. They should mark each difference with a circle on the right-hand picture.

Pirate flag

Photocopy the Pirate flag template, 6.8 (p. 156), for each child and ask them to design their own pirate flag on it. Tell them to be as imaginative as they can.

Captain Bartholomew Roberts

Photocopy the Captain Bartholomew Roberts template, 6.9 (p. 157), for each child.

Active games

Organise a pirate party session at the end of the week. The children can play the following games.

Pin on Pirate Pete's patch

Draw a large pirate face on card (or ask a child to do this) and cut out an eye-patch. Blindfold each child in turn. Let them have a go at putting the eye-patch in the correct position, using Blu-Tack®.

Musical islands

Place a sheet of paper or carpet square on the ground for each child. Play music, during which time the children mill around the islands. When the music stops, the children must find an island to stand on. Each time they stop, remove one or more islands. Any child without an island to stand on is out. Continue until you have a winner.

Musical pirate statues

While music plays, the children pretend to be engaged in pirate activities (no fighting allowed). When the music stops, they must freeze in a suitable pirate pose. The last person to freeze is out, as is anyone who moves. Continue until you have a winner.

Musical markers

Each child is a pirate, and has a strip of material which they tuck into their waist-band at the back. Each pirate must try to capture the strips of others while retaining their own. After several minutes, stop the action to see who has the most.

Musical coins

Place a table in the middle of the room and scatter 'coins' over the surface. These could be counters or any other suitable round object. Make sure there are enough counters for each child to have one. When the music plays, the children walk around the table. When the music stops, they pick up a coin from the table. After the first go, remove one or more coins each time. Any child without a coin is out. Continue until you have a winner.

Pirate hat

Enlarge the Pirate hat template, 6.10 (p. 158), and cut two hat pieces from folded black sugar paper for each child. Measure the hats around each child's head and staple the pieces together to fit. The children can either add a skull and crossbones badge from the template to the front or design their own. The children could wear their hats to a pirate party (see below).

Ahoy, me hearties

The children stand in an inward-facing circle. One child stands in the middle, wearing a blindfold. This child is turned several times and then raises their arm to point. The child in the circle who is being pointed at must disguise their voice and say "Ahoy, me hearties". The child wearing the blindfold has two attempts to guess the identity of the speaker. Repeat with a different child in the centre. You can ask the children in the circle to swap places occasionally to change their positions.

The children could bring in some items of food and give them pirate names (e.g. crisps could be scurvy skin flakes and grapes could be dead men's eyeballs). They could wear their pirate hats (see template 6.10, p. 158) while they eat the food.

Art

Pirate ship and pirates

Enlarge the Pirate ship and pirates template, 6.11 (p. 159), then cut two halves of a pirate ship from cardboard and three strips of card, bending the flaps along the dotted lines. The flaps are then glued to the inside of the ship halves to join them together. The children can add masts, sails and a pirate flag to the ship if they wish. Let each child make a pirate using a toilet roll centre as a body. They should attach a pirate head, arms and feet cut from card and any accessories they choose – such as a sword, a dagger and a pistol. Place all the pirates into the ship and make one a captain.

Treasure

The children could make coins, necklaces, bracelets, goblets etc from air drying clay then paint them gold and silver and arrange them in a 'treasure chest'.

Short story

What is inside the treasure chest and to whom does it belong?

What is special about this island?

Whom is this boy hiding from and why?

What is happening on board the ship?

Describe what's inside this cave.

Who is the captain of the pirate ship? Describe him.

Who has walked the plank and why?

Continue the pattern

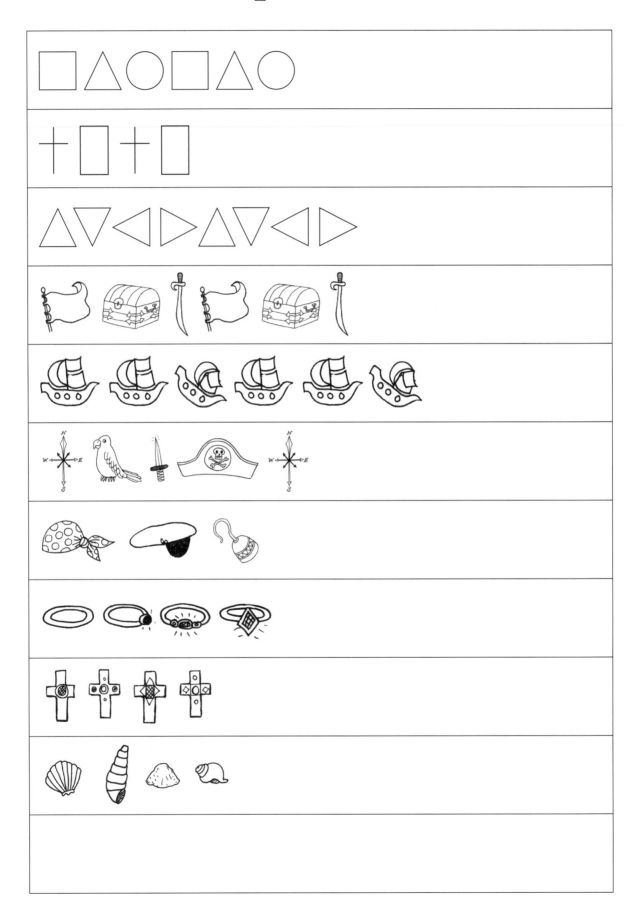

Pirate sums

1 Pirate Pete has a) 12, b) 35, c) 164 pieces of gold. He captures another a) 13, b) 47, c) 259. How many pieces of gold does he have altogether?

2 The six crewmen of *The Good Fortune* ask Captain Roberts for a) 2, b) 5, c) 13 bottles of rum each. How many bottles of rum must the Captain give altogether?

3 Barnacle Bill has a) 25, b) 74, c) 356 pearls. Shifty Sam steals a) 12, b) 37, c) 179. How many pearls does Barnacle Bill have left?

4 Cut-throat Jake has to share the treasure of a) 16, b) 64, c) 152 gold bars between eight pirates. How many gold bars does each pirate receive?

5 It takes Captain Cutlass the following lengths of time to sail between islands on his way to Africa. How many years and months does the whole journey take?
a) 3 months, 7 months, 5 months; b) 8 months, 13 months, 11 months; c) 15 months, 26 months, 18 months, 21 months.

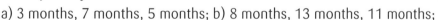

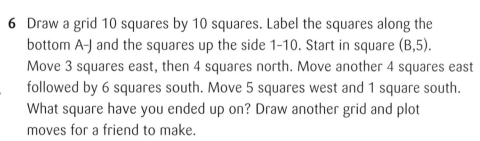

6 Draw a grid 10 squares by 10 squares. Label the squares along the bottom A–J and the squares up the side 1–10. Start in square (B,5). Move 3 squares east, then 4 squares north. Move another 4 squares east followed by 6 squares south. Move 5 squares west and 1 square south. What square have you ended up on? Draw another grid and plot moves for a friend to make.

7 Plot the following course that the *Merry Mermaid* sailed. Use a scale of 1cm to represent 10 miles. Sail 20 miles due east, then change course and sail 60 miles in a north-easterly direction, followed by 30 miles due east. Take a southerly direction for 70 miles, followed by 30 miles north east. Change direction again and sail 40 miles south west and then 10 miles due south. How many miles and in which direction will you have to sail to get back to your starting point?

Treasure Island

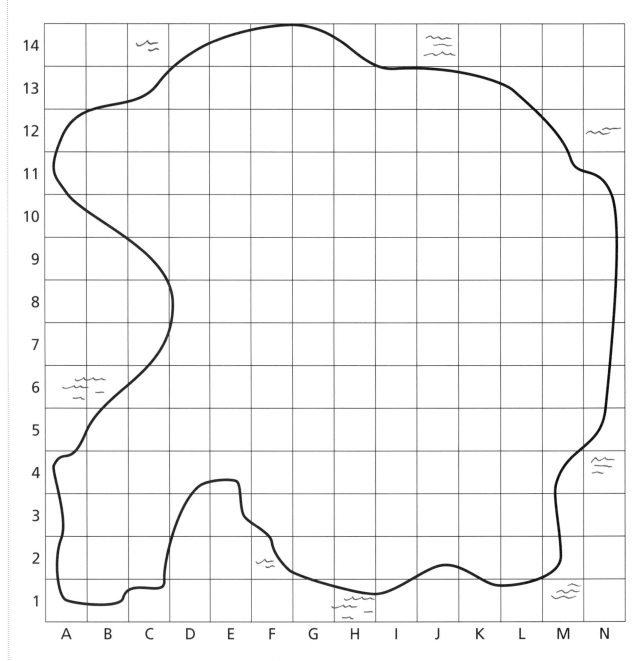

Draw the features below on the coordinates given.

 shark-infested waters (B,13)

 volcano (J,8)

 Navy men o' war (E,2) and (M,13)

 well (K,5)

 smuggler's cove (B,9)

 cave (N,7)

 mountains (D,10) and (D,12)

 shady spot (G,13)

 Navy fort (L,3)

 wild animals (G,8)

 Skull Rock (B,4)

 waterfall (M,9)

 pirate ship (B,7)

 hangman's noose (H,4)

 Snake Pass (D,11)

 man trap (J,3)

 look-out point (A,1)

 pirate store (D,7)

 lake (I,11)

Treasure chest

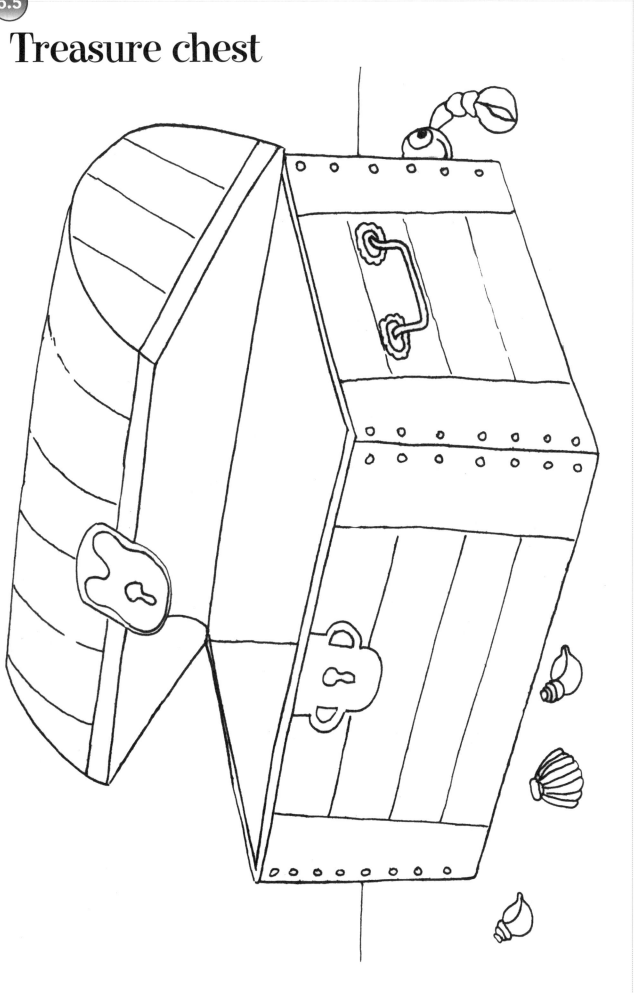

Pirate board game

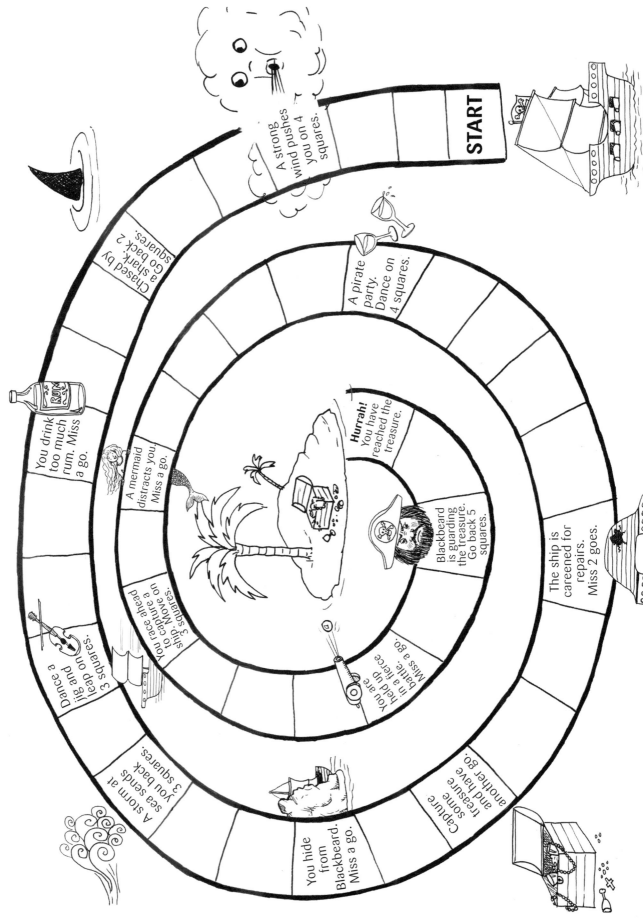

START

A strong wind pushes you on 4 squares.

Chased by a shark. Go back 2 squares.

A pirate party. Dance on 4 squares.

You drink too much rum. Miss a go.

A mermaid distracts you. Miss a go.

Hurrah! You have reached the treasure.

Blackbeard is guarding the treasure. Go back 5 squares.

The ship is careened for repairs. Miss 2 goes.

You are held up in a fierce battle. Miss a go.

You race ahead to. Move on 3 squares. You capture a ship.

Dance a jig and leap on 3 squares.

A storm at sea sends you back 3 squares.

You hide from Blackbeard. Miss a go.

Capture some treasure and have another go.

6.7

Spot the difference

Pirate flag

Design your own pirate flag. Some things that you could include are shown below.

Captain Bartholomew Roberts

Colour the picture of the pirate captain

Pirate hat

Place on fold

Pirate ship and pirates

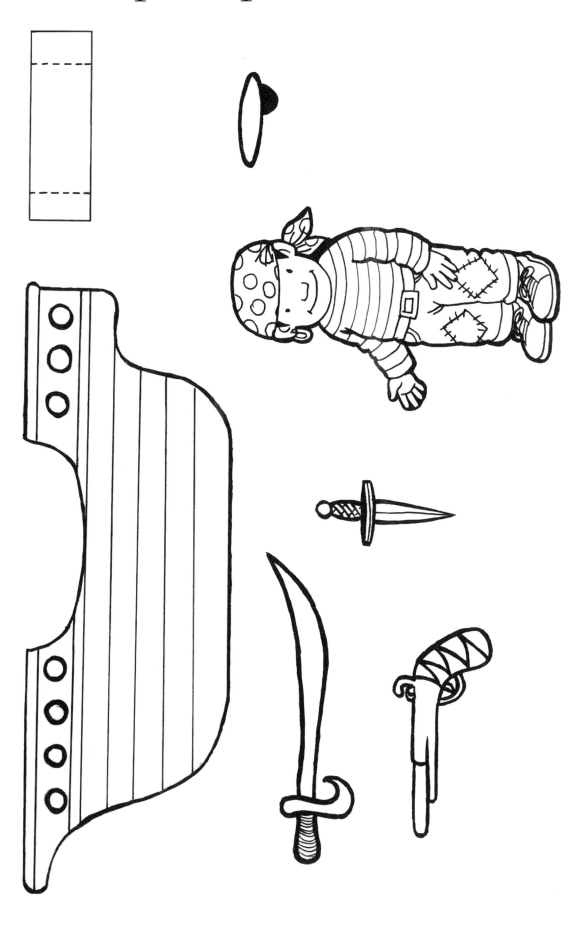

Permission to Photocopy

Answers

Story 1

1.5 *A garden message* (p. 28)
What is your favourite thing in a garden?
What is bigger a mouse or an ant?

1.6 *Follow the clues* (p. 29)
Go to: deckchair (4), fence (14), runner bean (7),
paddling pool (2), wheelbarrow (11), swing (15),
pond (17), bird table (1), carrots (6), tree (16), garden
gnome (18), spade (8), marrows (5), pots (9), nest (3),
watering can (12), shed (10), frog (19), flower bed (20),
greenhouse (13).

Letters in box: ELROWF = FLOWER

Story 2

2.3 *Space crossword* (p. 50)
Across 2 Spacesuit, 3 Saturn, 5 Planets, 9 Star,
11 Astronaut, 13 Atmosphere, 14 Alien, 15 Off,
17 Moon, 18 Rocket, 20 Milky Way, 21 Simulator,
23 Galaxy, 24 Mercury, 25 Gravity, 26 Cone,
27 Astronomy

Down 1 Jupiter, 2 Stand by, 4 Test, 6 Earth,
7 Satellite, 8 Mars, 10 Race, 12 Leo, 15 Orbit,
16 Solar system, 19 Thrust, 21 Summer, 22 Launch

2.4 *Space quiz* (p. 51)
sweets, rugby, apple, mouse SRAM = MARS
orange, owl, night, monkey OONM = MOON
pig, clouds, ant, egg, slipper / hot, ice, soft, pip
PCAES/HISP = SPACESHIP

2.5 *Find the space words* (p. 52)
1 VENUS, 2 ALIEN, 3 METEOR, 4 ROCKET, 5 JUPITER,
6 SHOOTING STAR, 7 MILKY WAY, 8 SPACE/SHIP

2.6 *Space missions* (p. 53)
A circles = 36, stars = 89; B circles = 44,
stars = 91; C circles = 45, stars = 94

Story 3

3.1 *Find the hidden message* (p. 72)
The cat is black
The witch flew out on her broomstick on Halloween

3.4 *The wizard's journey* (p. 75)
wand (7,5), elf (14,10), glass slipper (5,9), witch (3,4),
potion (9,8), magic tree (14,1), broomstick (6,12),
fairy (11,5), cauldron (4,15), cat (2,11)

The remaining four are: cloak (2,14), spell book (9,2),
ring (10,12), dragon (12,14)

3.6 *Complete the magic squares* (p. 77)

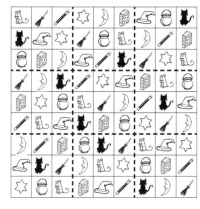

Story 4

4.2 *Aztec maths* (p. 97)
1. a) 8, b) 22, c) 44 d) 61 e) 425 f) 883
2. a) 22 + 6 = 28 b) 41 + 23 = 64 c) 25 − 3 = 22
   d) 12 + 30 = 42   e) 43 + 22 = 65 f) 43 − 5 = 38
3. a) 423 + 442 = 865   b) 802 + 46 = 848
   c) 464 − 123 = 341   d) 843 − 421 = 422

4.6 *Journey through the desert* (p. 101)
a) 1 hour 10 minutes, b) 3 hours 30 minutes.

4.11 *Aztec fishermen* (p. 106)
B has caught the fish

Story 5

5.1 *Around the world map* (p. 124)
(C,10) skier, (P,6) tiger, (V,2) sheep, (H,5) cocoa bean,
(K,8) sun cream, (T,11) walrus, (D,9) grizzly bear,
(N,6) oil, (R,8) panda, (G,5) tree, (M,7) pyramid,
(K,12) whale, (S,10) chopsticks, (F,8) burger,
(Q,11) Russian hat, (U,3) surfer, (F,11) alligator,
(L,9) bicycle, (M,3) diamond, (S,4) kangaroo,
(J,8) dolphin, (F,6) Mexican hat, (M,11) Father Christmas,
(R,5) palm tree, (P,4) oil tanker, (L,10) fish, (K,7) camel,
(M,5) lion, (Q,9) Great Wall, (T,3) snake, (O,10) Russian
doll, (M,6) elephant, (K,9) the Queen, (H,3) beef cattle

Story 6

6.3 *Pirate sums* (p. 151)
1 a) 25, b) 82, c) 423
2 a) 12, b) 30, c) 78
3 a) 13, b) 37, c) 177
4 a) 2, b) 8, c) 19
5 a) 1 year 3 months, b) 2 years 8 months,
  c) 6 years 8 months
6 D2
7 60 miles north west